LIFE IN THE THREE SIXTH GRADES

John H. Lounsbury
J. Howard Johnston

National Association of Secondary School Principals
Reston, Virginia

Scott D. Thomson, *Executive Director*
Thomas F. Koerner, *Editor and Director of Publications*
Carol Bruce, *Associate Director of Publications*
Eugenia Cooper Potter, *Project Editor*

National Association of Secondary School Principals
1904 Association Drive, Reston, Virginia 22091
(703) 860-0200

ISBN 0-88210-212-5

Contents

Acknowledgments

In order to provide the base data for this project, 132 observers gave a full working day of their lives without recompense. For this service they deserve special thanks. These educators accepted our directions and our date and willingly participated as observers and recorders. The significant contribution of the 23 analysts is also worthy of recognition. Each of these individuals received a group of approximately 20 studies along with directions for conducting the analysis which involved careful reading, re-reading, and deliberation. The members of both these important groups are listed in the Appendices.

Joel Milgram, University of Cincinnati, prepared the foundation chapter on the nature of sixth graders. For this we are much in his debt.

The cooperation of hundreds of teachers and principals in the schools visited should not go unrecognized. Without their willing support the study would not have been possible.

In addition, two individuals provided the day to day administrative support so essential to conducting such an extensive study. George Melton, deputy executive director of the National Association of Secondary School Principals, and Kathleen Thurlow, secretary, spent endless hours corresponding, recording, duplicating, and distributing. Their management of the administrative aspects of this project are greatly appreciated.

Mary Mitchell was responsible for typing and retyping as drafts became a full manuscript and her yeoman service is recognized with appreciation.

For taking this report in manuscript form and turning it into a professional publication, NASSP's editorial office deserves special thanks.

All told, hundreds of individuals contributed something to this study. They either gave encouragement, assistance, approval, time, study, or special skill of some sort. If the results are of any value these persons deserve some credit. The writers who reviewed all the studies, the analysts' reports, and related literature, and who prepared this document, accept full responsibility for any shortcomings.

John H. Lounsbury
J. Howard Johnston

CHAPTER 1

The Sixth Grade:
Caught in the Middle

T he sixth grade reflects more diversity in organizational arrangements than any other grade in the K-12 continuum. In grades 7 and above departmentalization has had a virtual hammerlock on schools. In grades 5 and below the self-contained classroom has been by far the most prevalent practice. But in recent years, one is likely to find departmentalization, teaming in any one of its many variations, or the self-contained approach being used in sixth grade classrooms.

Even the school unit in which the sixth grade is located may not indicate the type of instructional organization employed. An increasing number of elementary schools departmentalize the upper grades while a few middle schools maintain an almost self-contained classroom in the sixth grade. The sixth grade, then, is both literally and figuratively caught in the middle of the K-12 public school continuum, lost between or buffeted between elementary education and secondary education. It has not always been so.

For more than 80 years, since the graded structure with its ladder concept was first implemented, the sixth grade was firmly ensconced as a part of elementary education. Sixth grade, in everyone's view, was simply one part of the grammar school. Even after the movement to reorganize secondary education, which began in the 1910s and which led to the creation of the junior high school, had robbed elementary education of grades 7 and 8 the place of the sixth grade seemed secure.

But in the 1960s the middle school was introduced and a new wave of school reorganization began rolling across the land. A central feature of this educational innovation was a school organizational pattern that placed the sixth grade in an intermediate unit in a 5-3-4 plan. (Some middle school leaders even advocated a 4-4-4 plan.) In the last 25 years sixth grades by the hundreds have thus been incorporated into middle level units. In fact, the shift has been so extensive that the 5-3-4 plan is now the most common single form of school organization in the United States, replacing the older 6-3-3 pattern which had held the top spot for some 40 years.

Yet, the number of sixth grades still found within elementary units is substantial and no complete demise of such an arrangement is expected in the fore-

1

seeable future. Other sixth grades continue to be housed in K-12 and other comprehensive units of organization. So sixth grades may be located in elementary schools, middle level schools, or in some other grade configuration.

Since middle level education, despite its widespread existence, has not gained acceptance as one of three distinctive levels of education, those sixth grades that are located in elementary schools operate under the aegis of elementary supervision and administration, whereas those sixth grades found in intermediate level units almost always fall under the control of a secondary education division.

Obviously the rationale, approach, and practices of elementary and secondary education differ—yet sixth graders are of the same age regardless of the school unit in which they are housed. At age 11 or 12 they are not just children nor are they yet adolescents. So the questions—Are elementary programs and practices too "childish" for emerging adolescents? Are secondary programs and practices generally inappropriate for young people still not adolescents?—are pertinent.

It is time to take a careful look at the place of the sixth grade in public education. In many respects it has been the victim of organizational and administrative decisions rather than the cause of those decisions. Neither elementary nor secondary education has taken an adequately active stance concerning the nature of the school program that should be provided for these young people who are just moving out of childhood and taking the first steps toward adolescence.

The study reported here was designed to address three specific questions: (1) What is a sixth grader's day in school really like? (2) In what ways do the programs provided sixth graders differ, depending on where that grade is located in the school system? and (3) How does our knowledge of the nature and needs of sixth graders match up with the program actually provided?

The Plan of the Study

The study was patterned after NASSP's ninth grade project, *How Fares the Ninth Grade?*, which was completed in 1985. The data for the present study were gathered during the first observance of National Middle Level Education Week, March 7-14, 1987, using the "shadow study" technique. Observers shadowed randomly selected sixth graders during the entire school day of Wednesday, March 11. Using a simple form and following a limited set of directions observers made a record of the events and activities of each individual student, completed a brief general information sheet, and conducted an end-of-the-day interview with the student.

In addition, observers summarized their findings and reactions and completed a previously sealed checklist of program characteristics. Copies of the shadow studies, together with the other materials, were returned to NASSP. (Appendix B describes in more detail the technique and includes copies of the forms used.)

Each NASSP state representative to the Middle Level Committee was asked to conduct a study and to secure one other person from his or her state. In addition, members of the Middle Level Committee completed a study as did a number of individuals who had asked to participate or who responded to the invitation in the *NewsLeader*.

An orientation period for volunteers was held at the time of the open meeting of the Middle Level Committee during the San Antonio Convention. All necessary forms and related information were distributed at that time. Individuals not present were mailed complete directions and materials.

The total analysis was planned to be essentially three-fold: (1) to determine, in a generalized fashion, the nature of the sixth grade program in the United States as it exists from the standpoint of the consumer; (2) to discern how the programs provided appear to reflect and meet the nature and needs of sixth graders; and (3) to ascertain the ways in which sixth grade programs differ according to their placement in the school organization scheme.

Three categories of schools were established: (1) those in which the sixth grade was the entry grade, (2) those in which the sixth grade was an internal grade, and (3) those in which the sixth grade was the terminal grade.

After the studies were logged in, the survey sheets and checklists were set apart. The studies were then duplicated and packs of randomly selected studies, with identifying data removed, were mailed to members of a panel of analysts.

To conduct the initial analysis of the studies submitted a panel of 23 educators was selected. Principals, teachers, and teacher educators were included on the panel. Each analyst received 18 to 20 shadow studies, randomly selected, along with suggestions and guidelines for carrying out the analysis. To help ensure a fair analysis, each individual shadow study was included in three different packets and thus was read by three different educators.

The comparative aspect of the study employed a checklist of program characteristics that were deemed desirable in a sixth grade. This list, developed by the Middle Level Council and validated by members of the analyst panel, was given to the observers in a sealed envelope so as not to influence their observations. Following completion of the shadow study and the individual's reaction to it, observers opened the envelope and completed the checklist indicating the degree to which the sixth grade program they observed seemed to evidence these conditions and characteristics.

The checklists were placed in one of the three categories, tabulated, and the results statistically analyzed to determine the differences in school programs that might be attributed to the placement of the sixth grade. In order to provide a further analysis, the studies were also categorized by instructional organization (self-contained, departmentalized, and teamed) and additional comparisons made.

The entire group of shadow studies, the analysts' reports, the general information sheets, and the tabulated checklists were available to the authors during their preparation of this final written report.

Altogether, 132 studies were completed and constitute the data base for this study. These studies were made in 45 different states. Sixty-one studies were done in schools where the sixth grade was the entry grade, 50 were in schools where the sixth grade was the highest or terminal grade, and the remaining 21 were in comprehensive schools where the sixth grade was an internal grade.

While the students selected to be shadowed were chosen in a random manner, the schools do not constitute a true random sample. They were simply those schools available to the volunteer observers and thus can only be identified as a

3

representative group of sixth grades.

Though limitations exist and some desired scientific technicalities could not be met, taken together the studies and the reports constitute a powerful body of data. These snapshots of reality reveal much about the ways sixth grade students are being educated. Serious consideration of the findings is warranted.

Drawing generalizations is always a risky business. Few of us, however, can resist the temptation to derive an apparently evident conclusion from some number of cases. While risky, the pursuit of generalizations is an important matter, for lessons to help understand present conditions and to direct future activities are derived from this procedure. In fact, the improvement of education is highly dependent upon generalizations.

Education, which involves complex human beings on both sides of the desk is, however, particularly hard pressed to derive scientific, unchallenged conclusions from even its most tightly controlled research studies. In the present study, the authors were cautious in drawing conclusions, as the sixth grade studies defied easy generalizations.

A major reason for this is, in itself, a generalization about the sixth grade that has considerable importance. It is because, as noted earlier, the sixth grade in the United States displays such a variety of organizational and instructional arrangements that generalizations about the total grade are somewhat limited in number. The educational implications of this condition are many.

As the studies and the analysts' reports were read it became apparent that it was difficult to draw a detailed single picture of life in the sixth grade, to make generalizations that were representative of clear majority practices. What became evident was that there are, in fact, three sixth grades, each identifiable and fairly distinct but not based on the school administrative unit in which the grade is located.

The first is the traditional sixth grade, self-contained and elementary in nature and form. It is a single class group instructed in all or almost all the basic subjects and skills by one teacher. This teacher assumes responsibility for students' behavior and personal development as well as providing formal instruction. Many such sixth grades continue to exist, but not just in elementary schools. Essentially self-contained sixth grades are occasionally found in middle schools.

The second is the departmentalized sixth grade, secondary in nature and form. A student group moves from class to class to receive instruction from different specialist teachers. This plan has been invading upper elementary schools for many years, even before the middle school movement became influential, so the school unit in which a departmentalized sixth grade is located may not be a middle level school.

The third sixth grade is the evolving sixth grade, the teamed sixth grade. There instruction in the basic subjects is provided by a team of two to five teachers, each with some subject area expertise, but who may plan the total instructional program cooperatively. Sometimes the subjects are correlated or fused and occasionally a thematic unit may be pursued by the team. While the teamed sixth grade is fairly distinct from the other two basic plans, it covers a wide range as far as the degree of interdisciplinary implementation goes. In all too many cases, while a team has been organizationally established, departmentalized instruction continues. In other cases two or more teachers teach the basic subjects and plan together closely.

4

This concept of the three sixth grades will be used at many points in this report as a way of drawing pertinent conclusions and making contrasts.

At the same time, there are numerous statements that can be made about sixth grades *in general*. Readers should be reminded, however, that the studies do include examples of almost any condition and generalizations that are derived from the group cannot be viewed as describing any one school or all sixth grades. The studies quoted and the reactions cited in this final report readily reveal the range in quality that exists among sixth grades.

The second chapter in this monograph provides a description of sixth graders, their nature and needs. Readers would be well-advised to review this foundation material for it provides the ultimate yardstick against which to measure the appropriateness of school programs. An appreciation of the nature and needs of these diverse beings should be fresh in one's mind as the reports on what is happening in their classrooms are reviewed.

The third chapter presents the study's findings as they grew out of the analysts' reports as well as the authors' reading of the studies. Supportive notations from both observers' reactions and analysts' reports are often cited. The perceptions of students as revealed in the end-of-the-day interviews are also summarized in this chapter.

Chapter 4 presents the findings as derived from a full analysis of the checklist data along with some demographic data. When treated statistically, these data were able to answer, at least partially, questions about whether the organizational unit in which a sixth grade is located affects the program offered. Likewise, comparisons between the three sixth grades were possible and are reported in this chapter. Related conclusions are included in this chapter.

Chapter 5 is composed of seven complete shadow studies supplemented by some additional observer reactions. Readers may want to read these studies before delving into the results as viewed by the analysts and authors, as the seven studies present a substantial sample of the data.

The final chapter presents major conclusions and related recommendations. Several related research studies are cited in Appendix A. An elaboration of the shadow study technique comprises Appendix B with listings of the observers, schools, and analysts following.

CHAPTER 2

The Sixth Grader:
A Profile*

A sixth grader is someone who is often reminded by a teacher that she is no longer a child and should act accordingly. Sixth graders are also reminded by seventh graders that they are not yet teenagers and should not try to act as if they were. And 17-year-olds who work at the local movie theater selling tickets will remind the sixth grader that if the twelfth birthday has come and gone adult prices must be paid to gain entrance to the show.

Sixth graders are, in part, what other people perceive them to be. Schools, adolescents, and commercial establishments all contribute to the perception of what a sixth grader is—and the messages are muddled.

Do sixth graders know what they are? Hardly. Their own self-perception is shaken by the onset of the physical changes that have just begun and will soon accelerate at a frightening pace. "Get hold of yourselves," the physical education teacher shouted to a class of 12-year-olds who were having some difficulty in settling down. But how does one get hold of oneself when oneself keeps changing so quickly?

If the 35-year-old physical education teacher looked at a photograph of himself taken three years before he would view a very recognizable individual. The changes, if any, would be minor; maybe a few more pounds here and there and maybe a little more tired looking, but that's about it. But when we ask a sixth grader to look at a photograph of herself taken three years earlier what does she see? A third grader who bears little resemblance to the 11 or 12-year-old! How can one possibly know one's own self if the self doesn't hang around long enough to be recognized?

What is a sixth grader? We give them a label so we can discuss them and study them. We call them pre-adolescents but, as the late Hershel Thornburg reminded us, is there really any comfort in being *pre anything*? Nevertheless, that's what they are—on the verge of adolescence but not adolescents. This suggests that the sixth grader has special needs that must be attended to.

Transitional periods in the life cycle have an integrity all their own. The pre-adolescent stage has its own unique characteristics demanding certain kinds of responses from the schools in order to help ensure a safe and healthy passage to

*This chapter was written by Joel Milgram of the University of Cincinnati.

adolescence. Some of these unique characteristics are examined in the following sections.

Physical Development

The growth in height is the most dramatic and obvious change that happens to the sixth grader—well, not all sixth graders, for while the rapid growth starts at age 11 for girls it is not until 13 for boys. This means that starting in the sixth grade (and continuing through the seventh) many of the girls will be several inches taller than their male counterparts. One should not underestimate the social impact this has upon the 12-year-old.

For many years boys and girls have observed that most husbands are taller than their wives, that most football players are taller than the female cheerleaders, and that most leading men in Hollywood are taller than their leading ladies. Should they view a movie where this is not true (Woody Allen being a frequent example) it turns out that the film is a comedy! No one likes to involuntarily be a part of a comedy but to some extent the differential growth rate at this age plunges both boys and girls into the theater of the absurd. All are equally self-conscious. The boys fear the loss of their manhood even though it is not yet theirs to loose. The girls wonder if they will be condemned to be giants in a world of male dwarfs. Undoubtedly they will all survive but the sympathetic understanding of the schools can make it a lot easier. Lining them up in size places is not the kindest act to perform!

Of course, there are other physical changes taking place. Breast development in girls is one of the more obvious secondary sex characteristics, and it is very obvious to the boys who invariably will comment among themselves as to the relative breast sizes in the class. The boys will also comment, but only to themselves, as to the amount of pubic hair they have or do not have. Within the same sex the rate of physical development varies greatly. Puberty, though seemingly sudden, is actually a continuation of the growth of the body that began at birth.

Reaching puberty is a major benchmark in the life cycle. Some girls will menstruate when they are 8 years old and some will not until they are 16, but the average age in this country is just over 12. So in the sixth grade many schools will march the girls into a room, without boys, to see THE FILM. After the film a woman teacher will look at her watch indicating there is little time left and ask if there are any questions. Since there are none, the girls will return to their classes to deal with the snickering boys and their provocative questions. The following day most girls will come to school with well-stuffed purses and the boys will snicker once more.

Unfortunately for too many sixth graders that is just about all the information their schools will provide them about their bodies and the rapid changes that are taking place. Others will be more fortunate, attending schools where the curriculum includes units that inform children about their bodies and prepare them for the changes certain to come. In either case it is a confusing time for the 11 and 12-year-old and will remain confusing for the next several years.

Social Development

One of the factors that influences the social development of the sixth grader   7 is their reconceptualization of the status of the significant adults in their lives. Parents who were always wise and omnipresent now appear to be more fallible. It now seems possible to do some things without parents finding out about it. Though they are still useful in assisting with homework (or insisting that they help with homework) parents seem to be having difficulty in some of the subjects, especially math and science.

Teachers, too, are viewed differently. They are not able to control everyone as they seemed able to do back in the fourth grade. Sixth graders see other sixth graders actually defying teachers' commands, and the human qualities of teachers become more apparent. This changing view of other adults coincides with the growing need to develop friendships and the growing dependency on those friendships.

We often remind our students that they are not in class to socialize. We are wrong, of course, for they *are* there to socialize. It is their developmental right to socialize, something they must learn how to do as one of the major tasks of pre-adolescence. Besides, parents become parents without asking the child's permission and teachers are assigned in an equally authoritarian manner. *Friends represent choice.* Friends represent the vehicle through which independence asserts itself. Peer relationships, therefore, start to become, in the sixth grade, the number one priority for many youngsters. This means that the fifth grader who always did his homework on time and studied hard for all tests may, as a sixth grader, place greater priority on successful socialization at the expense of lower grades.

How should teachers react to this new priority? Teachers do not like to see study habits disintegrate and intellectual pursuits take a back seat to socialization. Yet, it is important to understand and be sympathetic to the strong need of the 11 and 12-year-old to seek out and maintain friendships. From their perspective such activities are more important than math and social studies. Teachers must remind themselves they are only part of students' lives, an essential part to be sure, but they must share the stage with the many other developmental tasks that are part of pre-adolescence.

The friendship patterns at this age reflect a marked increase in experimentation and exploration. Friendships may cross over racial and economic boundaries for the first time in an effort to decrease the dependency on family values. It is also an age to play with various social sex roles. Boys will "dress tough" one week and look quite conventional the next. Girls will appear (or attempt to appear) seductive on Monday but then look like Alice-Blue-Gown on Friday. To conclude that they simply cannot make up their minds as to which image they want to portray is only partially correct. It's actually a sophisticated process of measuring audience reaction. When a sixth grader dresses a certain way you can be sure he or she is observing everyone's reactions and making a personal decision as to which kind of reaction is most satisfying.

Schools that allow for plenty of opportunities for socialization are viewed as nice places to be by the students. It is wrong to assume, however, that schools provide time for socialization only in the lunchroom and on the playground. Classroom discussions and other group activities also allow for social interactions. The need of pre-adolescents to interact with one another can be satisfied within the context of a lesson on improper fractions.

Emotional Development

Along with the physical and social development of this age group the increased variability of the sixth graders' emotional status becomes evident. Life is definitely more complicated for these students as they try to balance the various and often contradictory expectations of parents, teachers, and friends. Though children of this age often work hard to demonstrate an increased autonomy they are still very dependent on adults for emotional support. This increased autonomy is often misinterpreted by teachers and parents as a statement of emotional independence.

It has been suggested that first grade teachers smile more than sixth grade teachers because the upper grade students don't need that many smiles! The reverse is probably true. The pre-adolescent feels less secure in many areas than his younger counterpart and is certainly more confused about the many changes that are taking place within himself and his peers. It is a time when compassion and understanding are absolutely necessary for healthy emotional development.

The mood swings that are observed in many children of their age are, in part, due to hormonal changes in their bodies. It is also tied to the increasing complexity of their social interactions. The interactions we observe in the classroom are only a small part of their relationships. Friendships continue after school and the quality of the after-school relationships affect the next day's behavior in class. For the 11 or 12-year-old, the telephone can directly affect one's self-esteem. Phoning and being phoned help determine one's acceptability and therefore one's emotional status. Parents who are overly critical about grades or behavior or appearances clearly contribute to feelings about oneself. There is little that happens after school that doesn't affect what happens in school. Schools that provide ample opportunities for pre-adolescents to express their emotions, directly or indirectly, are providing a necessary component for healthy psychological growth.

Interaction of Characteristics

Some general observations of the characteristics stated above are in order. It is easy to be misled into believing that the sixth grader deals with physical development followed by social development, followed by emotional development. The order of things is a writer's convenience and bears no relationship to the facts of life. The 11 or 12-year-old deals with all these states of being simultaneously. They interact upon each other constantly often making it difficult, if not impossible, to isolate one from the other.

To add to the confusion there is frequently little coordination in the growth of these characteristics; one can be physically mature and emotionally and socially immature. The reverse can also be true. Teachers are often confused by this lack of coordination in growth. Too often a physically mature sixth grade boy will be given a task he is too emotionally immature to handle. A socially mature girl will be thought to be socially immature because of her immature physical development.

Despite all these difficult aspects of pre-adolescence, most sixth graders handle themselves very well. A school, however, can make their transitional stage from childhood to adolescence considerably easier or much harder.

9

Summary of sixth graders' characteristics and conditions surrounding them

1. Sixth graders receive contradictory information as to whether they are children or adolescents.

2. They are changing at a dramatic rate and many of them feel their bodies are going in the wrong direction.

3. They are extremely self-conscious about these changes. Few adults will talk to them about it.

4. Teachers and parents are now known not to be infallible. Twelve-year-olds cannot always get teachers and parents to admit this.

5. There is a strong need for socialization at all times. Socialization is a developmental right.

6. Socialization needs and learning are not mutually exclusive.

7. The opportunity for independence is needed.

8. There is still an emotional dependence on adults. Smiles and encouragement are necessary.

9. Friendships may have a greater priority than grades.

10. Social experimentation and exploration is typical and healthy.

11. After-school interactions directly affect the next day's school behavior.

12. Talking about moods and other emotions is healthy and opportunities to do so are desirable.

13. The interactions of social, emotional, and physical growth happen in a simultaneous and uncoordinated fashion.

14. Schools are capable of helping significantly or hindering seriously the development of sixth graders.

15. Pre-adolescents need to take risks and fail with dignity.

16. The need to participate is important regardless of one's level of skill. This applies to sports as well as academic activities.

17. A disliked teacher will become a loved teacher if that teacher lets the child know he is prized.

18. Knowing the capital city of the 50 states is less important than the child's perception that his or her school is an emotionally safe place to be.

19. Sixth graders have a need for teachers who understand what it is like to be a sixth grader.

Do the sixth graders around the country attend schools that respond to their needs? The results of the shadow studies described in the following chapters will help us find the answer.

CHAPTER 3

Life in the Three Sixth Grades

M arch 8-14, 1987, was designated as National Middle Level Education Week. Sponsored by NASSP's Middle Level Council, it was the first such celebration. During that week several activities took place to mark the occasion. A Middle Level Conference was held in Washington, D.C. Governors of 33 states issued proclamations. And on Wednesday, March 11, more than 100 sixth graders were "shadowed" and their activities recorded to provide the data for this study.

The study was initially designed, among other things, to compare differences between sixth grades that were the terminal grade (K-6), the entry grade (6-8), or an internal grade (K-12). During the analysis by the authors it became apparent, however, that the more critical differences, in many respects, were in the way the grade was organized for instruction rather than in the school unit in which the grade was located. Departmentalized sixth grades differed markedly in a number of ways from self-contained sixth grades, wherever they were located. The same is true of teamed sixth grades. Sixth grades located in elementary schools might use any one of the major organizational patterns while middle schools were almost always either teamed or departmentalized.

Although analysts were given randomly mixed groups of studies they regularly sensed and reacted to the differences that were apparent in the organizational approach. Attention was thus shifted in the authors' final analysis to these latter differences as well as to differences that might be attributed to administrative unit locale.

In the most extreme form of generalizing these quick assessments could be made relative to the basic differences that emerged. In self-contained sixth grades students sit for long periods of time doing seatwork. In departmentalized sixth grades students sit for long periods of time listening to teachers. In teamed sixth grades no single generalization is possible as either of the above conditions may be prevalent as well as various interim conditions.

Other generalizations that appeared in the shadow study reports concerning these three instructional arrangements follow.

Teachers in self-contained sixth grades seemed less concerned with discipline, permitted more student movement within the class, gave greater attention

11

to individuals, and gave students more choices. There was more flexibility in the use of time and in the seating arrangements employed. Limited attention to exploration or exploratory areas was evident.

Opportunities for student involvement in clubs and special activities were infrequent and/or limited in scope. Content coverage was somewhat less obvious while skill instruction was quite apparent. The school day itself in self-contained sixth grades appeared to be markedly shorter.

Teachers in departmentalized situations seemed more preoccupied with control and behavior, engaged in more whole-class activities, and lectured more frequently. The focus of activities was largely on the covering of content *per se* with little or no relationship to the developmental needs or current interests of the students.

Teamed situations cover a continuum from departmentalization on the one end to nearly self-contained classrooms on the other with both ends overlapping the other groups. Generally, however, very limited utilization of the interdisciplinary instructional opportunities provided by teaming was evident.

The General Nature of Sixth Grade Programs

The guidelines provided to the analysts identified 12 aspects of a school program. Their reports, in part, were built around these headings and they are used here as a framework for summarizing the nature of school experiences sixth graders underwent in March of 1987. Specific statements of observers and analysts are included in parentheses, frequently as examples of the evidence supporting the generalizations. Additional insights on the nature of sixth grade programs are provided in the following chapter, which analyzes the demographic and checklist data.

A. *Curriculum Content (Subject Matter)*

Sixth graders are heavily involved in learning the basic, standard subjects. The "big four" plus reading are almost always present. And the subjects are usually presented in the traditional separate subject manner regardless of the organization in place.

There were many references by observers and analysts alike to the lack of examples of relating content to the realities of students' lives in the present. ("No evidence of content related to the world." Analyst. "Very little relation to world outside school—communism, acid rain, and current events magazine are three isolated examples." Analyst. "Only A/A was truly relevant." Analyst.) Likewise, observers and analysts noted that there was almost no evidence of one subject being related to another. ("Not once was there a note on interrelating anything." Analyst. "There is virtually no integration of content or school activities for sixth graders." Analyst.)

A heavy reliance on the textbook and individual seatwork was most apparent. The transmission of information was the specific focus of most activities. The limited attention to geography and health was noted by more than one analyst and observer.

The lack of opportunities to explore new topics or content was frequently cited. Only in those schools with specific exploratory courses was much exploration going on. ("This experience helped to convince me that sixth graders do need exploratory experiences. They do not need the length of time that we schedule for academics. They seem to need 'hands-on' experiences and the opportunity to experience things through more than quiet listening." Observer.) Exceptions were noted in science and in social studies projects. Some observers felt that even the exploratory courses, when provided, were too narrow.

B. *Teaching Arrangements*

Taken as a whole, sixth grades cover the gamut as far as the ways they are organized for instruction. Wholly self-contained save for music and physical education all the way to fully departmentalized situations with a variety of blocks, partial teaming, and variations thereof can be found.

The school unit in which the grade is located is not a certain indicator of instructional organization, although it does indicate the most likely pattern. If a grade is self-contained it is almost always in an elementary unit. In the schools sampled in this study there was only one self-contained unit in a middle level institution. Full departmentalization is most likely to be found in a middle school. Only a few of the fully departmentalized sixth grades in this study were located in elementary units. The predominant arrangement, teaming in some form, is frequently found in an elementary unit as well as in a middle unit. Generally, however, sixth grades in elementary units tend to employ two or three person teams rather than four or five person teams.

Language arts and reading were frequently blocked. Ability grouping was heavily used in mathematics and reading classes. In departmentalized grades ability grouping was sometimes used across the board.

C. *Instruction and Teaching Methods*

Teacher-directed large-group instruction covering textbook material describes the most prevalent instructional approach found. ("It was rare for teachers to break away from whole-class activities." Analyst.) One observer described the academic routine as "little more than read this and answer that."

Disappointing to many observers and analysts was the notable absence of interdisciplinary instruction or even simple correlation. ("One concern is the 'disjointedness' of the school days described. Rarely do activities in any one class relate to activities in another. From a student's point of view, the school day must seem like a long series of unrelated 'blips', messages that may be important but are never connected." Analyst. "I was a bit dismayed that even though this student's teachers are organized as interdisciplinary team teachers there is little crossover from one subject to the other. For the most part the day is fragmented. . ." Observer.)

When relationships between subjects were noted it was most likely to occur in self-contained situations. ("The daily schedule [self-contained] was smooth. Subject changes were an easy transition as location did not change." Observer. "A great deal of continuity between classes. The learning of one class carried on through the day. There was only one real separation of coursework and that was when a special music teacher came in. This was also the least effective hour of the day." Observer.)

The passivity of students was frequently cited as a major concern. So, too, was the lack of any real involvement of the students in the teaching-learning 13 process. ("The instruction promoted passive learning rather than interactive learning. . ." Analyst. "Students talked when given permission but for the most part were very passive." Analyst. "Students were passive—watching, listening, reading except in PE and Art." Analyst.)

The traditional routine of checking homework, explanation of new materials, individual work on related problems or questions, brief discussion or quiz, and assignment of homework was very much present in these sixth grades.

Lecturing was particularly prevalent in departmental and teaming situations while seatwork, usually well-monitored by teachers, was more abundant in self-contained classrooms. In neither case were problem-solving approaches or efforts to engender creative or critical thinking evident.

Instances of group work and cooperative learning were quite limited, but when they occurred it was most likely to be in an essentially self-contained class. ("Subject-centeredness predominates in these classes with most active learning and student-centered activity appearing to occur in self-contained settings." Analyst.)

The use of games was quite common and appeared to be effective in generating student interest. ("I noted how well sixth graders react whenever a game is played. I am convinced that teachers can call anything that they do a game and it will be well-received by sixth grade students." Observer.)

D. *Teacher-Student Interaction*

Almost all interactions between a teacher and a student centered around the content. Observers and analysts often expressed disappointment at the almost complete absence of social or informal interaction between teacher and students. ("There is very little student-student or student-teacher interaction—a lot of quiet seatwork." Observer. "The noted instances of students talking with school adults was depressingly low." Analyst.)

At the same time, observers and analysts regularly noted the overall positive nature of the student-teacher relationship. ("Many observers were impressed with the warm, caring environment and positive attitudes of teachers and students." Analyst. "Students moved about freely, for the most part, and got to their classes on time, respected school officials, and demonstrated a sense of pride in their school." Observer.)

Discipline was seldom identified as a problem while the positive behavior of pupils was frequently noted. ("Boys and girls at random pick up bathroom pass. Hardly anyone is disruptive or disrupted. I was amazed. No one abused time to leave and return to room." Observer.) One questionable interaction resulted in this comment: "It's hard to believe that there are teachers who still ask kids to give their test grades out loud and embarrass them in front of their peers."

The overall behavior of the students leads one to conclude that sixth grade students, compared to seventh and eighth grade students, still respect the authority of the teacher and are less likely to challenge it.

E. *Student-Student Interaction*

Student-student interaction occurred frequently and consistently, though seldom because of the intent of the teacher. In their desire for socialization with peers sixth graders show clearly that they are emerging adolescents. Between classes, at recess, and at lunch student-student interaction was especially constant and spirited. ("Students communicated with peers using soft-talk, face-

14

making, or note passing." Analyst. "A whole 'world of communications' took place in the schools between students, and teachers did not seem to acknowledge or attend to these interactions—except when talking disrupted their class." Analyst.)

Several observers decried the lack of class-related interaction and the likelihood that some students could fall through the cracks. ("I think it's frightening that many of the quieter students could go through an entire day without interacting with more than one or two other students." Observer. "The need for more interaction, particularly during instruction, was mentioned by all observers in some manner." Analyst.)

While opportunities for student-student interaction relative to academics were scattered, there were a few examples. For instance, in one 6-8 school the record showed the science class divided into groups to test liquids with litmus paper. Two periods later in social studies the subject first worked with two classmates in a group and then studied for a tournament with several other students. The next period he worked at a computer with two other classmates.

Students with initiative, of course, created opportunities for social encounters, however brief. Visits to the waste basket or pencil sharpener were, obviously, as much for interaction with a friend as for their presumed functional purpose. ("In all cases, all students observed cultivated social encounters and interaction whether the school permitted it or not." Analyst.)

F. *Physical Environment*

While observers were not asked specifically to describe the physical environment, many did. In most cases the descriptions were positive. ("Attractive room, student work evident." Observer.) "Traditional" was another term used frequently to describe the furniture, its arrangement, or the general school environment. "In classic rows" was another apt description.

Self-contained classrooms seemed more likely to be furnished with tables and chairs or to have desks arranged in ways other than rows.

The age of the building was occasionally noted in negative terms, but the physical facilities provided sixth grade youth do not appear to be factors that hinder learning. One minor exception might have been that school in which a ceiling tile dropped into a student's lap—and the student was reprimanded for causing a disruption!

G. *Advising and Counseling*

Understandably there was limited specific evidence of advisement or counseling taking place with the shadowed students. Indications did exist, however, that several middle schools had scheduled advisory periods and some self-contained teachers appeared to assume limited guidance responsibilities. A reliance on the guidance specialist seemed to pervade thinking.

(Information on the availability of counselors will be found in Chapter 4.)

H. *Opportunities for Social Skill Learning*

Early adolescents are very much social beings. Their animated conversations and constant efforts to relate to others socially, however awkward and inappropriate those efforts may be, are evidence of their need to socialize. The shadow studies were filled with accounts of students interacting socially with others. Rarely, however, was this within an academic context or with teacher approval.

One analyst, a teacher, said "Not one of the observers mentioned any type of training in social skills! Where are kids to learn these skills if parents are too busy and teachers are worried about covering the required curriculum? We all know that they learn from peers in the hallway, in locker rooms, and the school cafeteria . . . in other words, they pick up each other's bad habits."

Another analyst pointed out that whenever this matter occurred teachers dealt with it as a reaction to a problem rather than as a preventive measure or learning opportunity. Another surmised, quite correctly, that such skills were taught indirectly by the behavior and conduct norms that were established and maintained.

It seems fair to conclude that, for the most part, sixth grade programs do not include direct, positive attention to developing the social skills of learners.

I. *Teacher and Student Use of Class Time*

Use of class time was largely controlled by the teachers. Classes were structured, students were busy. A number of observers commented on the efficiency of the teacher's organization. Many noted the ready availability of the teacher to help an individual. However, it appears that while the class may be busy many individual students in the class are off-task.

Seatwork, tests, copying, reading, were far more prevalent than discussing, reporting, or interacting in other ways. The lack of student involvement was mentioned time after time by both observers and analysts. ("The most disappointing finding was the seemingly large percentage of time when students were not engaged." Analyst.)

There were some exceptions—"An exciting science class." "A thrilling band trip." "Deeply engaged in a discussion with his group." But these exceptions only seemed to prove the rule—sixth grade for most is heavily filled with busy-work and passive activities. ("I was truly amazed at the amount of 'sitting' time and even more amazed how well students do at 'sitting'." Observer.)

Students do a lot of doodling, reading, drawing, to combat boredom during much class time. And, of course, they socialize surreptitiously.

A number of observers and analysts pointed out the drop in productivity that occurs in the afternoon. ("As the day moved on evidence showed that students were tired and less productive." Analyst. "All students in the United States start leaning on their elbows at 1:53 p.m.?!" Analyst.) The after-lunch slump with its decreased student attention is a reality.

J. *School Learning Climate (student and teacher attitude)*

In a word, "positive." Students and teachers generally evidenced good attitudes and satisfaction with their situations. Classrooms were apparently pleasant and warm. One analyst characterized the teacher attitude as "keeping house but being nice." Teachers evidenced concern and pupils reacted positively toward them with limited exceptions. One analyst characterized the climate as "neutral" and another felt that most environments were rather "joyless," but, by and large, the overall atmosphere in sixth grade classrooms does not seem to be a detriment to learning.

One analyst noted that evidence of positive attitudes in one class showed up all day in that school and vice versa. This, he felt, indicated that attitudes and behavior may reflect building leadership, staff morale, and overall climate more than differences among individual teachers or students.

16

The analysts provided many valuable insights based on their study of a group of shadow studies. These insights usually came in the general, open-ended response opportunity beyond the structured areas which were summarized above. Included here are a number of excerpts from these observations and judgments, mostly on topics not already discussed.

"The greatest need seemed to be in the areas of pedagogy and social interaction. It seems that these schools were interpreting the back to basics thrust in a manner similar to schools in general. Small, incremental activities emphasizing isolated responses seemed to create a sterile approach. There appeared to be very little 'right hemisphere' brain activities with creativity in evidence."

"Educators seem very concerned with being efficient and seem very unconcerned with being effective. They work hard doing the job right without considering whether the right job is being done.

"Lack of integration of subject matter and application to real life reinforce the idea/feeling of education as 'not the real world'."

"Having been a reader in the ninth grade study, I expected to feel better about the sixth grade reports. I do not. In fact, given what we know about youngsters at this grade, and with all the information available, it was very disappointing to read about the school day many of these students were expected to endure."

"It appears that there are many similarities between a sixth grader's day and a ninth grader's day, and I find this alarming. Rigid classroom expectations, heavy content, lots of seatwork, little socializing, and high expectations are difficult enough for ninth graders, but they almost seem too defeating for sixth graders.

"I found several instances in the reports where the observers mentioned they were bored and tired. I can just imagine how a sixth grader was feeling. I think part of my concern about this was that the students seemed to have developed a feeling that this was the way it should be and as students they seemed resigned to it."

"Based on these reports, it came through clearly once again that the teacher is the key factor in promoting and implementing a school's program. Despite a relatively rigid curriculum, an inflexible schedule, and lack of opportunities to explore and socialize, students saw the concern, interest, and humor of their teachers as the most important considerations in their school experience."

"As the observers indicated, the teacher seems to be the key variable. Some of them provide excitement, enrichment, support, and occasionally even joy. Others seem to act out the sentiment expressed by a teacher to one observer: 'I love teaching kids, but do not like my job.' They seem stifled by routine and unable to change things."

"There seemed to be a positive relationship between the teacher's willingness to allow students some control over procedural matters, rules, format, and time-lines and the amount of time students spend on-task. Teachers whose lessons called for a change of pace, a change of learning mode, and who modeled or had concrete examples of the product to be produced were more successful than were the more academically rigorous."

"I hate to think that sixth grade education in America is as dull, boring, and pedestrian as the reports I read would indicate. Many of these schools have obviously not learned about or utilized such concepts as decision making, lesson-planning models, cooperative learning, learning styles, or higher level thinking skills."

As the Students See It

At the end of the day each observer engaged the shadowed student in an interview using, in part, seven questions. The students' responses to these questions are summarized below.

1. When asked about the "good things" at their school, the most frequently cited thing was "the teachers." Eighteen of 23 students in self-contained classes included teachers in their lists, which constitutes a very positive response. No other single response matched in frequency the number of times teachers were listed as one of the three "good things" they would tell a new student.

The next most often cited thing was "friendly students." Principals were often identified as one of the good things.

Other things that appeared a number of times were: the gym, the building, the lunch room, choice of food in the cafeteria, intramural activities, changing classes, and interesting activities in some classes.

Students were often unable to identify things they would change if they could. Some said "nothing." "More time at lunch," "starting later," "less homework," "opportunity to eat in class," "bigger lockers," and air conditioning or heating were the sorts of things frequently cited—things that related to "creature comfort" rather than educational programs (not surprising, of course).

Obviously, students had not given much thought to this type of question.

3. When asked how they felt, in general, about their teachers sixth graders were highly complimentary. "They're nice." "Good." "Friendly." "Fair." "Explain things well." "Really nice." "Don't embarrass us." "Considerate." "Helpful." "I like them." "Understanding." The exceptions to very positive assessments were so infrequent as to "prove the rule." Most of those were rather neutral or mild. "They are alright." "They are okay, like a tipical (sic) teacher." "Some are mean." "Too strict" (strictness, however, was often cited as a positive

trait). "Talk too much."

In the eyes of their students, sixth grade teachers get high marks. About this, there should be no question. While professional observers may not be so complimentary, sixth graders have amazingly positive perceptions concerning their teachers.

4. When asked if there was a person in the school that they would readily turn to for help with a personal problem, students were less likely to name a teacher. However, it is worth noting that students in self-contained classes identified their teacher far more frequently than did students in teamed and departmentalized situations. In many cases, students would say, in effect, "a friend first, then a teacher." Some responded that there was no one in school they would turn to for help on a personal problem. More commonly, however, students identified the principal or a counselor if not a teacher.

5. Comments on their feelings about the way students treat one another were generally positive. Other students were usually judged to be friendly or nice. However, a good many responses also indicated concerns over a portion of the students who were "mean," "pushed other kids," "pick on some kids," "say bad things," or "fight too much."

6. Answers to the questions "How do you feel, in general, about your classes?" and "Do they challenge you?" were quite varied and specific. Overall, positive comments outweighed neutral and negative ones. Students often used the question to indicate a favorite class or claim that they are all okay except _____. Many sixth graders did indicate that they felt their classes could challenge them more, but such assessments were clearly in the minority.

7. The last interview question asked was, "Do you have opportunities to help make decisions about what goes on in class?" The consensus answer was "not really." Some specific and typical responses were: "Sometimes, in physical education class." "Pretty much decided by teacher." "No, day pretty well planned." "She lets us vote and if most of the class agrees, maybe she'll let us try it." "No, I just go along." "Yes, sometimes she will let us help with the rules." "Only when choosing report topics." "The teacher tells us what to do." "No, the teachers have to stay on their schedules." Reading the answers, and between the lines as well, it appears that sixth graders don't have any expectation that they should have such opportunities. When indicating they did have opportunities they cited relatively low level choices or simple options. The chance to vote on something was often mentioned.

While students have limited experiences against which to judge their school and program, their perceptions have real importance simply because they are the basis for their attitudes and behavior. Fortunately, they are quite positive. It is interesting to note the usual discrepancies between students' positive perceptions of their school situations and the very critical judgments of those situations by professional observers. "Ignorance is bliss," that old maxim, may be something of a saving grace for educators.

CHAPTER 4

Descriptive and Comparative Analysis of Schools and Program Elements

E ven the most casual observer is struck by the wide variety of school and program arrangements that serve sixth grade students. When subjected to more systematic study, the differences remain, but patterns emerge that allow us to compare these programs with one another on some standard elements. That is the purpose of this chapter. In it, we present a description of the schools and programs that were studied. We also compare these school types and organizational patterns for the presence or absence of program elements and school characteristics that are generally accepted to be sound middle level practices.

A Description of the Sample

School Characteristics

First, the very *names* of schools that housed sixth graders varied. The sample contained elementary schools (33 percent), middle schools (64 percent), junior high schools (1.5 percent), and two K-12 schools (1.5 percent).

The grades housed in these schools were equally varied. Table 1 shows the grade configuations of the 132 schools included in the study.

These schools represented 45 states and all types of communities: cities, suburbs, small towns and villages, and regional schools in rural areas. The sample provides a reasonably accurate picture of the kinds of schools that are provided for sixth graders in the United States. It also closely parallels recent national statistics.

The sizes of the schools were also variable. They ranged from a small school of 162 students to a 1,650-student giant. The average school size was 597 students.

Organizational patterns were variable as well. About 30 percent of the schools used a self-contained format, 9 percent had some form of block-of-time schedule, 34 percent employed interdisciplinary teams to some degree, and 24 percent of the sample was composed of departmentalized sixth grade classes.

Table 1

Number and Percent of Schools in Sample Representing Each Grade Configuration

Grade Configuration	Number	%
4 - 6	1	.8
5 - 6	4	3.0
5 - 7	1	.8
5 - 8	6	4.5
6 - 7	6	4.5
6 - 8	54	40.9
6 - 12	1	.8
K - 6	47	35.6
K - 8	3	2.3
K - 12	2	1.5
3 - 8	1	.8
3 - 7	1	.8
6 only	1	.8
4 - 8	2	1.5
not identified	2	1.5

Over three-quarters of the sixth graders in the study (82 percent) had access to a professional counselor in their schools. The ratio of students to counselor was very disparate, however. In one school there were only 99 students for each counselor; in the worst case, there were 1,889 per counselor (a 900-student school with a half-time counselor). The average number of students served by each counselor was 481; the median was 401.

Program Elements

Virtually all the students had access to, and in fact participated in, some kind of interest-centered activity outside normal classes. More than two-thirds of the students (68 percent) had access to more than two of the following options: clubs, mini-courses, sports, or electives. All but 2 percent had access to at least one or two of these interest-centered activities.

Average class size varied tremendously, from a low of 17 students per class to a high of 34. The average for all school types and organizational plans was 26.5 students per class. The median is also 26.5, indicating that the distribution of class enrollments is virtually normal throughout the sample.

What do our sixth graders study? There was considerable variation in the subjects actually studied as a function of the instructional organization employed in the building, but most of us who attended school in the 1940s, '50s, or '60s would recognize the names of the courses taken by students today. Table 2 shows the percentage of students who were enrolled in each of the following subjects. While this type of sampling does not describe the total school program experienced by students over the course of the year, it does provide a picture of the kinds of learning experiences a student might have on a typical day.

Somewhat surprising is the relatively smaller number of students taking science. Evidently, science is not taught quite as routinely or regularly as are the other "core" subjects of English, math, and social studies. In fact, a larger number of students (91 percent) in this sample are likely to take formal reading instruction than a science class.

21

Table 2

Percentage of Students Enrolled in Each Subject/Course

Course	%	Course	%	Course	%
English	98	Reading	91	Art	43
Soc. Studies	96	For. Lang.	9	Music	54
Math	96	Computers	23	Home Econ.	12
Science	87	Phys. Educ.	82	Ind. Arts	11

In general, sixth graders are not likely to study foreign language, home economics, or industrial arts. Art and music are much more common electives, and some form of computer instruction is also growing in popularity. Physical education remains a substantial part of the program for sixth graders, and is nearly as likely to be taught as is science.

Program Practices and Characteristics

In addition to gathering a very limited amount of demographic data and some information on program elements, each of the site visitors completed a checklist that contained 23 program components that had been identified as being desirable in an effective program for young adolescents. The presence or absence of each of these elements was noted on the form that appears below (Figure A). Each rater determined if there was "little or no evidence," "some evidence," or "ample evidence" that the program condition was in place in the school they visited. For the most part, this meant that the student they shadowed actually participated in the practice during the day of the study, but the fact that these judgments are highly subjective is acknowledged. Once again, a one-day observation does not accurately reflect an entire program *for any one school;* however, this sample of reality does give some indication of the relative prevalence of a number of school practices in sixth grade classrooms throughout the sample. It appears that observers were somewhat more critical in their open-ended narrative reactions, as reported in the previous chapter, than they were in completing the checklist.

Based on checklist data, several conclusions can be drawn about the kind of programs that sixth graders are experiencing on a day-to-day basis.

First, approximately 64 percent of the raters reported "some" or "ample" evidence of the existence of a teacher adviser or home-based guidance program. At the same time, while a large number of students had access to a counselor in the building, in only half the schools was there "ample evidence" of counseling services.

For most sixth graders, interest-centered programs were available and utilized. More than three-quarters (77 percent) of the raters said that there was some or ample evidence of opportunities for students to participate in interest-centered activities either in or outside class. A somewhat smaller number (57 percent) said that there was evidence of clubs or related organizations in which all students might elect to participate.

The existence of basic exploratory programs was most evident. Nearly 81 percent of all students received some instruction in one or more of the basic exploratory areas, although relatively few (less than 50 percent) received instruction in various aspects of physical growth, including sexual development.

Figure A

*Presence or Absence of Selected Middle Level Program
Practices and Conditions, Indicating Percentage of
Raters Who Identified Each Practice*

<u>Program Characteristics or Conditions in the Sixth Grade</u>

It is recognized, of course, that while no evidence of a condition may be apparent on one day, such a condition may exist. Respond, however, based on your single day's observation by checking in the appropriate column.

1 = little or no evidence that the condition is present
2 = some evidence that the program condition is present
3 = ample evidence that the program condition is present

	Little 1 %	Some 2 %	Ample 3 %
1. Was there evidence of a teacher-adviser or home-base teacher who had clear guidance responsibilities for individual students?	36	26	38
2. Was a professional counselor available to sixth grade students when they needed personal assistance?	26	23	51
3. Did the student have an opportunity to participate in some interest-centered activities?	23	44	33
4. Were clubs or related organizations in which all students might participate available?	43	24	33
5. Were varied print and non-print media readily available and used?	12	33	56
6. Did teachers seem to use appropriate diagnostic information about student developmental characteristics, learning styles, and skill levels?	17	52	31
7. Did teachers use a variety of methods and approaches?	14	42	44
8. Was instruction in various aspects of physical growth, including sexual development, provided?	58	25	17
9. Was information in the areas of sex, alcohol and drugs, and related health concerns provided under appropriate adult leadership?	50	27	22
10. Did the student receive instruction in one or more of the basic exploratory areas of art, music, industrial arts, and homemaking?	20	19	61
11. Did the student participate in instructional groups of various sizes (full class, small group, pairs, large group)?	20	26	54

23

		Little 1 %	Some 2 %	Ample 3 %
12. Did the student participate in instructional groups of different types (homogeneous, heterogeneous, interest centered)?		19	37	45
13. Did the day include any experiences that addressed the personal-social needs of students?		34	32	34
14. Did the student receive direct instruction in skill areas such as reading or writing?		11	14	75
15. Were separate subjects correlated or fused in instruction?		34	45	21
16. Was the subject matter studied related to "here and now," to the present lives of students?		20	42	38
17. Did the physical education activities recognize and accommodate the varied levels of development?		34	32	35
18. Did the student participate in an intramural activity?		73	13	14
19. Was the community utilized as a resource, either by a resource person, field trip, or related activity?		62	20	19
20. Was the student recognized individually (addressed directly by name) by (a) at least one teacher during the day? (b) three or more teachers?	(a) (b)	7 8	7 6	86 80
21. Did student-teacher planning occur during the day, or was student input sought on any phase of school operations?		55	30	15
22. Was the student involved in situations calling for value discrimination, critical thinking, or analysis of options?		32	38	30
23. Did the day include any opportunity for interaction with students of other grade levels?		57	19	24

Slightly more students (49 percent) received some instruction on sex, alcohol, drugs, and related health concerns, but the number was still not great on this "typical" school day. The results on the extent to which the program addressed the personal-social needs of the students were mixed, with nearly a third of the observations falling into each category: little evidence, some evidence, or ample evidence.

There was evidence (83 percent found some or ample) that teachers seemed to use appropriate diagnostic information in planning instruction, and 86 percent found some or ample evidence that teachers used a variety of instructional approaches with the sixth grade classes. A wide variety of media were used, and

89 percent of the raters saw at least some evidence of the use of both print and non-print media in instruction.

Students tended to participate in different sized groups for instruction, and slightly over 80 percent of the raters saw evidence of that practice. They were almost equally likely to participate in different *kinds* of groups: heterogeneous ability, homogeneous ability, interest centered, or self-selected. Grouping patterns tended to change throughout the day.

According to the raters, nearly 91 percent of the students received some or ample direct instruction in skill areas such as reading or writing, a figure that correlates with the percentage of students who had direct reading instruction during the day.

Most raters (80 percent) found some evidence of specific attempts to relate subject matter to the "here and now" concerns of students, while only about two-thirds (66 percent) noted any attempts to correlate or "fuse" the different subjects studied during the day. Despite attempts at relevance, more than 60 percent of the raters did not note any attempt to use the community as an instructional resource for sixth graders. Further, relatively little evidence (55 percent) of student participation in planning was seen, nor was student input widely sought in any phase of the school day. A surprisingly large number of students, almost a third, were judged not to have been involved in decisions that called for value discrimination, critical thinking, or analysis of options during the day.

Students shadowed were recognized individually and addressed directly by at least one teacher during the day (92 percent). In fact, almost the same number of the students (92 percent) were addressed directly by name by three or more teachers during the day. Relatively few (43 percent) had any interaction with students from other grade levels during the day.

Physical education programs were evenly divided in the extent to which they recognized the unique development of individuals in the programs. Approximately one-third showed no evidence of such recognition, one-third showed some, and one-third showed ample evidence. A large number of students (73 percent) did not participate in any form of intramural activity.

Descriptive and Comparative Analysis
Based on Placement of Sixth Grade in
School Sequence

Almost since the advent of the middle school, a debate has raged over whether the sixth grade belongs as the last grade in an elementary unit, the first grade in a middle level unit, or in some other organizational location. In this section, we explore the apparent effect these different placements have on school characteristics and program elements.

School Characteristics

Grade placement is related, in a moderate degree, to school size. In schools where the sixth grade is the last of the sequence, the average school size was 532 students (range: 239 to 1,360); in middle level schools where the sixth grade was the first in the school, the average school size was 672 students (range: 162 to 1,650). In schools where the sixth grade is neither the first nor the last grade in the school, such as a 4-8 plan, or a K-8 organization, the average size of the school was 472, with a range of 217 to 1,005 students.

Schools with essentially elementary organizations—grade configurations ending with the sixth grade—were somewhat smaller than middle level schools, and schools where the sixth grade was in the middle of the grade span were the smallest of all. In the latter case, schools with many grades in them (K-8, 4-12, etc.) tend to be in smaller communities; therefore, the student population is likely to be somewhat lower as well.

Somewhat surprisingly, class size did not reflect the overall size of the school. Average class sizes were virtually identical for all sixth graders. Both in schools where the sixth was the entry grade and where it was the exit grade, the average class size was 26.5, with a range of 17-34 and 18-33 respectively. In schools where the sixth was the middle grade, the average class size was 25.7, with a range of 20-30. Given the size of the sample, this small difference is neither statistically nor practically significant.

The grade configuration itself is of interest because of the variety that exists. Table l, presented earlier, shows the distribution of school organization types included in the present analysis.

As expected, school organization was clearly related to the ways in which students were organized for instruction. There was a higher proportion of self-contained classes in the schools where sixth was the exit grade and a higher concentration of interdisciplinary teams or academic departmentalization in schools where sixth was the entrance grade. Patterns for schools where sixth was a middle grade were quite variable. Table 3 shows the results of this comparison.

Table 3

Instructional Organization in Schools
Where Sixth Grade Is Entry, Exit, or Middle Grade

Organization	Entry	Exit	Middle
Interdisciplinary Teams	46%	21%	25%
Self-Contained	7	56	44
Blocked	15	4	6
Departmentalized	31	14	25

Clearly, interdisciplinary teaming is the most popular instructional organization in middle level school, with departmentalization following in popularity. In elementary organizations, self-contained classes are most prevalent for sixth graders, with teaming second. In other grade configurations, self-contained plans are most common, with teaming and departmentalization tied in second place.

Middle level organizations have a moderate advantage over other plans in the activities they offer. Table 4 shows the relationship between grade placement and the school's activity program.

As expected, middle level schools offer a somewhat more comprehensive activity program, although both other school types do offer activities for sixth graders in the building. This may reflect both the specific attention to the activity program that is recommended in most middle school literature *and* the generally larger size of middle level schools, with accompanying greater resources for activity programs.

Table 4

Student Activities as a Function
of Placement of Sixth Grade as First, Middle, or Last

Type of Activity	First	Last	Middle
Clubs	10%	21%	33%
Mini-Courses	8	4	0
Sports	3	8	13
Electives	2	0	0
Comprehensive (More than 2)	77	4	53

Counselors are much more prevalent in middle schools than in schools where the sixth is the terminal grade in the building, and somewhat more common than in schools where the sixth grade is in the middle of the grade organization plan. In middle level schools (entry sixth grade) more than 93 percent have a professional counselor in the building; in elementary organizations (terminal sixth grade), only 67 percent have professional counselors. In those schools where the sixth grade occurs in the middle of the grade range, just over 80 percent have professional counselors, many of those in the schools which have a middle or secondary configuration (grades 4-8, 3-7, 5-7, 3-8, and 6th grade only). At the same time, these data show the increasing presence of professional counselors in elementary schools, a most encouraging trend.

Do students in these three types of schools encounter a different curriculum? With several notable exceptions, the curriculum is fairly standard across school types. Table 5 shows which subjects are taken by students in each school type.

From this table, it is clear that virtually all students take English and social studies, although students in schools with a terminal sixth grade are slightly less likely to be enrolled in social studies. Virtually all students in sixth grade entry and sixth grade terminal schools take math, whereas only 88 percent of sixth graders in schools with the sixth grade in the middle took math on shadow study day. Results for science were slightly more variable, with more than 90 percent of the students in sixth grade entry schools taking science, 84 percent in sixth grade terminal schools, and 88 percent in mid-point sixth grade schools enrolled in science. Reading was most commonly taught in sixth grade terminal schools, and least likely to be taught, directly, in schools with a mid-point sixth grade.

Foreign language, while not common in any of the organizations, is more likely to appear in a school with a mid-point sixth grade, and least likely to be offered in an elementary organization. Computer studies of some form are present, almost equally, in all three school types, as is physical education.

Art and music are most likely to be offered in a school with a terminal sixth grade, and least prevalent in schools with an entry sixth grade. The extent of the exploratory offerings in elementary schools, however, may not be as great. Home economics and industrial arts are virtually nonexistent in elementary organizations (sixth grade terminal), and most common in middle level schools where the sixth grade is the entry grade.

Table 5

Courses Taken by Sixth Graders in Schools
Where Sixth Is First, Middle, or Last Grade in Building

Subject	First	Middle	Last
English	98	100	98
Social Studies	98	100	94
Math	98	88	98
Science	90	88	84
Reading	90	81	98
Foreign Language	10	12	10
Computers	23	25	23
Physical Education	82	81	84
Art	36	44	52
Music	44	56	67
Home Economics	23	12	0
Industrial Arts	20	12	2

In short, courses that require specialized facilities and special teachers, except for art and music, are less likely to be offered in sixth grade terminal schools. Reduced offerings of art and music in middle level schools seems to be an artifact of the generally richer exploratory programs offered in these schools, where sixth graders are also likely to study home economics and industrial arts and technology. Computer science is firmly established as a legitimate subject in all these schools, evidently supplanting foreign language study as a popular exploratory option.

A potentially alarming trend away from specialized instruction in science and mathematics is suggested in these data, a trend that seems to be slightly more prevalent in elementary organizations than in middle level or mid-point sixth grade schools. Reading, however, is more likely to be taught in sixth grade terminal schools, a trade-off that is predictable when one considers the relative amount of preparation elementary teachers receive to teach language arts as opposed to science and mathematics.

Program Practices and Characteristics

The present data set enabled us to examine differences in program characteristics and conditions that could be attributed to the placement of the sixth grade in the building. As in the previous section of this chapter, raters assessed the presence or absence of program characteristics associated with successful middle level education programs. Figure B presents the results of this rating.

From these data, it is clear that major program differences emerge, some quite sharply, others with less certainty. The first area in which differences are noted is in guidance and counseling services. There was more evidence of a teacher-adviser or home base program in schools where the sixth grade is the terminal grade than in either sixth grade entry schools or schools with the sixth grade in the middle of the grade span. This appears to contradict a finding reported later in which self-contained classes, the most prevalent form in sixth grade terminal schools, had *less* teacher-advisory activity.

Presence or Absence of Selected Middle Level Program
Practices and Conditions, Indicating Percentage of
Raters Who Identified Each Practice

Program Characteristics or Conditions in the Sixth Grade
by Placement of Sixth Grade as First,
Middle, or Last in Building

It is recognized, of course, that while no evidence of a condition may be apparent on one day, such a condition may exist. Respond, however, based on your
single day's observation by checking in the appropriate column.

1 = little or no evidence that the condition is present
2 = some evidence that the program condition is present
3 = ample evidence that the program condition is present

		Little 1 %	Some 2 %	Ample 3 %
1. Was there evidence of a teacher-adviser or home-base teacher who had clear guidance responsibilities for individual students?	(L) (F) (M)	35 43 25	19 25 43	46 32 31
2. Was a professional counselor available to sixth grade students when they needed personal assistance?	(L) (F) (M)	43 12 25	19 28 25	37 60 50
3. Did the student have an opportunity to participate in some interest-centered activities?	(L) (F) (M)	27 19 25	42 45 44	31 36 31
4. Were clubs or related organizations in which all students might participate available?	(L) (F) (M)	58 29 50	23 22 25	19 48 25
5. Were varied print and non-print media readily available and used?	(L) (F) (M)	14 10 12	35 29 38	51 60 50
6. Did teachers seem to use appropriate diagnostic information about student developmental characteristics, learning styles, and skill levels?	(L) (F) (M)	12 23 18	58 40 69	30 37 12
7. Did teachers use a variety of methods and approaches?	(L) (F) (M)	15 12 19	35 45 50	50 43 31
8. Was instruction in various aspects of physical growth, including sexual development, provided?	(L) (F) (M)	62 52 64	23 27 29	15 21 7
9. Was information in the areas of sex, alcohol and drugs, and related health concerns provided under appropriate adult leadership?	(L) (F) (M)	56 47 50	27 27 36	17 27 14

		Little 1 %	Some 2 %	Ample 3 %
10. Did the student receive instruction in one or more of the basic exploratory areas of art, music, industrial arts, and homemaking?	(L) (F) (M)	33 9 21	21 17 21	46 74 57
11. Did the student participate in instructional groups of various sizes (full class, small group, pairs, large group)?	(L) (F) (M)	23 16 25	12 36 38	65 48 31
12. Did the student participate in instructional groups of different types (homogeneous, heterogeneous, interest centered)?	(L) (F) (M)	19 14 38	27 42 44	54 44 18
13. Did the day include any experiences which addressed the personal-social needs of students?	(L) (F) (M)	39 29 31	35 29 31	25 42 38
14. Did the student receive direct instruction in skill areas such as reading or writing?	(L) (F) (M)	14 7 19	12 19 6	75 74 75
15. Were separate subjects correlated or fused in instruction?	(L) (F) (M)	27 46 13	46 40 69	27 14 18
16. Was the subject matter studied related to "here and now," to the present lives of students?	(L) (F) (M)	19 22 20	42 45 33	39 33 47
17. Did the physical education activities recognize and accommodate the varied levels of development?	(L) (F) (M)	42 23 39	29 37 31	29 41 30
18. Did the student participate in an intramural activity?	(L) (F) (M)	65 77 87	16 12 13	20 12 0
19. Was the community utilized as a resource, either by a resource person, field trip, or related activity?	(L) (F) (M)	64 66 50	20 15 36	16 20 14
20. Was the student recognized individually (a) (addressed directly by name) by (a) at least one teacher during the day? (b) three or more teachers? (b)	(L) (F) (M) (L) (F) (M)	4 12 0 10 7 6	9 5 8 14 - -	87 88 92 76 93 80
21. Did student-teacher planning occur during the day, or was student input sought on any phase of school operations?	(L) (F) (M)	54 59 56	30 23 38	16 18 6
22. Was the student involved in situations calling for value discrimination, critical thinking, or analysis of options?	(L) (F) (M)	29 37 25	40 37 37	31 26 38

	Little 1 %	Some 2 %	Ample 3 %
23. Did the day include any opportunity for (L)	52	23	25
interaction with students of other grade (F)	60	16	27
levels? (M)	56	19	25

It is likely, too, that the matter of the guidance or advisory program is very different and more informal in elementary schools. Closer examination reveals that advisory programs seem to be a function of instructional organization rather than grade placement, and are more common in teamed and departmentalized arrangements than in self-contained groups. The percentage of terminal sixth grade schools with ample evidence of teacher-based advisory programs (46 percent) is almost equivalent to the percentage of these schools with teamed or departmentalized structures (40 percent). Evidently, it is the distribution of instructional organizational types that affects the presence of advisory programs in this data set.

As expected, schools with an entry sixth grade had substantially more evidence of professional counseling services (60 percent) than either terminal sixth grade schools (37 percent) or mid-point sixth grade schools (50 percent).

In all cases, observers found evidence that students had the opportunity to participate in interest-centered activities during the school day. However, sixth grade entry schools, or middle level schools, had substantially more clubs and related organizations for students (48 percent ample) than either sixth grade terminal schools (19 percent) or schools with the sixth grade in the middle of the grade range (25 percent). Predictably, students in middle level schools were also much more likely to have instruction in basic exploratory areas (item 10) than either elementary organized schools or mid-point sixth grade schools.

Instructionally, teachers were slightly more likely in the sixth grade entry school to use a variety of print and non-print media than in schools where the sixth grade was a middle or terminal grade. They were also slightly more likely to use appropriate diagnostic information than teachers in either of the other school types, although they and mid-point sixth grade schools were a bit less likely than terminal sixth grade schools to use a variety of teaching methods. Instructional variety, however, seemed to be provided for most of the students in the study, with very few of the observers noting "little evidence" of such variety in any of the settings.

Sixth graders in schools where they are the terminal grade or a middle grade are slightly less likely than students in entry sixth grade schools to receive instruction in various aspects of physical growth and development, or instruction related to sex, alcohol, and drugs. Further, students in middle level schools had experiences that addressed their personal-social growth needs (item 13) somewhat more frequently than students in other school types. This general trend is reinforced in the data analysis that follows, where team-taught classes, the most prevalent type in entry sixth grade schools, are more likely to examine these issues than other instructional organizations.

Grouping appears to be a bit more flexible in schools where the sixth grade is the terminal grade. In this sample, these sixth graders were more likely to participate in groups of different sizes than students in schools where the sixth grade was the entry grade or where it was a middle grade. In addition, students in the terminal sixth grade schools found themselves in groups of different types (homogeneous by ability, heterogeneous ability, interest, etc.) more often than students from either of the other schools.

Sixth graders in all school types were equally likely to experience direct instruction in basic skill areas such as reading and writing, but students in schools where the sixth grade was the entry grade were somewhat less likely to have a curriculum where separate subjects were correlated or fused in instruction. In fact, in no case was such curricular integration prevalent.

Students in schools where the sixth grade occurred in the middle of the grade distribution could expect a curriculum that was more closely related to the "here and now" concerns of young adolescents, although all schools seemed to make a reasonable effort in that direction. This ability to link learning to the lives of students may be a function of the relatively smaller size of schools where the sixth grade was placed in the middle; thus, teachers have a better opportunity to know both the students and the communities they serve. This observation is borne out by the fact that mid-point sixth grade schools were slightly more likely to use the community as a learning resource (item 19) than either of the other organizational types. This, too, points to a set of strong links between school and community most often found in smaller communities and schools.

Schools where the sixth grade was the entry grade seemed to provide more evidence of physical education programs that recognized and accommodated the developmental needs of young adolescents. However, all raters noted relatively little evidence of student participation in intramural activity, especially where the sixth grade is placed in the middle of the grade structure of the building.

Students were generally recognized and addressed individually by the teachers who work with them. Virtually all the students were recognized by at least one teacher, and in mid-point and entry sixth grade schools, most were recognized by three or more teachers on shadow study day. This finding is predictable, since many of the elementary organizations (terminal sixth grade) make use of self-contained classes, where students may not come in contact with many teachers during the day.

Only rarely were students involved in planning school or class operations in any of the school types. Most disturbing, though, is that sixth graders are provided with relatively few opportunities for value discrimination, critical thinking, or analysis of options. Schools where the sixth grade is either the final grade or in the middle of the grade range do a slightly better job than others, but active student intellectual engagement and critical thinking are not common practices in sixth grades included in this study. Finally, no school type seems to provide many opportunities for sixth graders to mix with students from other grade levels.

Comparative Analysis of Basic Organizational Plans

The data employed in this study enabled us to look for differences in both school variables and program variables across the three basic organizational types: interdisciplinary teams, departmentalization, and self-contained class-rooms. Interdisciplinary teams exist when the "core" subjects are taught by a team of teachers who share the same group of students and almost always the same planning period. Departmentalized systems provide for a subject specialist to teach his or her subject to several groups of students, who may or may not have any other teachers in common. No specific provision is made for teachers from different subject areas to share a common planning time, and teachers may or may not share the same group of students. In self-contained classes, one teacher is responsible for the bulk of instruction for one group of students each day. He or she teaches all the major subjects, although a specialist may be available for music, art, physical education, reading, or some other specific intervention program.

In order to identify potential differences among organizational types, each case was examined to determine the organizational category to which it belonged. In order to heighten the discrimination power of this analysis, relatively "pure" examples of each type were identified for the analysis. Since schools organized by teams differed so greatly in the degree to which they implemented interdisciplinary teaching, this large group was divided into two subgroups. Teamed schools were those that appeared to be clearly implementing the concept. Partially teamed schools were those that administratively were organized by teams but apparently were doing little interdisciplinary planning and teaching. This resulted in the following division of the sample:

Table 6

*Composition of Comparative Sample
by Organizational Type*

Organization Type	Number	%
Teamed	15	11
Partial Teamed	74	56
Self-Contained	25	19
Departmentalized	18	14

Clearly, schools that are pure examples of an organizational type are rare. Most make some use of both teaming and departmentalization. However, it was felt that it would be useful to identify the extent to which more nearly "true" examples employ specified middle level educational practices. This study provides the rare opportunity to engage in such a comparison with a substantial national sample of schools.

School Characteristics

The size of the schools varied somewhat by group. Self-contained and teamed schools were approximately the same size (average 670 students). Departmentalized schools and partially teamed schools averaged 490 and 564 students respectively. Evidently, little of a school's organizational plan can be attributed to student enrollment, with one possible exception. The smallest teamed school had 410 students in it, more than double the size of the smallest school in any other category. This would indicate that a certain critical mass of students is required for teaming to occur. At this point, however, that conclusion remains speculative.

Activities available for sixth graders are comparable across school types. The table below shows what percentage of schools offered the identified activities.

Table 7

*Percentage of Schools in Each Category Offering
Specified Activities for Students*

Activity	Teamed	Part Team	Dept.	Self-Contained
Clubs	7	23	6	17
Mini-Courses	13	4	11	0
Sports	7	7	6	4
Electives	7	0	0	0
Comprehensive	67	66	78	79

Although all schools offered activities for students, teamed and partially teamed schools seemed slightly less likely to offer a comprehensive program. This may result from the team of teachers, in many team arrangements, accepting the responsibility for providing team-based activities, rather than schoolwide activities. Thus, the program would appear less comprehensive to observers.

Teamed and departmentalized schools are more likely to have a professional counselor available to students (100 percent and 94 percent respectively), and partially teamed schools are usually staffed with counselors as well (83 percent). Self-contained schools are much less likely to have a professional counselor on the staff, as only 60 percent of the raters noted such a service in this category.

Counseling ratios, as one might expect from the data listed above vary in much the same way. Teamed schools have the lowest ratio (368:1), while departmentalized and partially teamed schools are virtually tied at 490:1 and 470:1, respectively. Because of the low number of counselors in self-contained schools, the ratios are higher, slightly over 670 students for each counselor.

Class size remained fairly constant throughout the sample. The average size of teamed classes is 26, exactly the same as for self-contained and partially teamed classes. Departmentalized classes are slightly smaller, at an average of 25.8.

Not surprisingly, the organizational arrangement *does* have an effect on the courses or subjects a student is likely to study. Table 8 shows the pattern of courses taken by students in each of the organizational plans.

All students in the teamed and departmentalized schools studied English, social studies, math, and reading on shadow study day. Nearly all the students in self-contained and partially teamed schools did as well. Science, however, is more likely to be taught in the teamed or departmentalized setting than in the self-contained class, and slightly more likely than in a partially teamed class. This may be attributable to the fact that self-contained teachers, who have the responsibility for teaching all the major subjects, may be less comfortable teaching science than the other courses, and just not do it so often. Furthermore, laboratory science is time-consuming, and some teachers may be unwilling to devote the time necessary at the expense of other subjects. In teamed or departmentalized schemes, however, there is usually no such choice. Either a science teacher lobbies to be sure that enough time is devoted to his or her subject, or a science class is actually scheduled on a regular basis.

Table 8
*Percentage of Students Taking Each Subject
on the Day of the Shadow Study
by Organizational Type*

Subject	Teamed	Part Team	Depart.	Self-Cont.
English	100	97	100	96
Social Studies	100	95	100	96
Math	100	95	100	96
Science	93	88	94	72
Reading	100	85	100	96
Foreign Language	7	12	6	4
Computer Ed.	20	28	17	12
Phys. Ed.	73	83	78	88
Art	33	44	33	56
Music	33	53	61	60
Home Economics	7	17	11	0
Industrial Arts	13	13	11	4

Physical education is somewhat more likely to be taught in self-contained classes and partially teamed classes than in either teamed or departmentalized settings. Art is also more likely to be taught in these settings, and music appears more in self-contained, departmentalized, and partially teamed settings than in teamed schools.

These findings suggest that teamed arrangments offer fewer of the standard exploratory courses than do the other configurations. However, because the raters found that there was "ample" evidence of student participation in exploratory areas in teamed schools, another interpretation is called for. Teamed schools may have more exploratory areas available to students; thus, they are less likely to be enrolled on any given day in the traditional exploratory areas listed on the instrument. It is possible that student exploration is conducted through a series of mini-courses or other arrangements that cycle students through a number of options during a year. In that case, the number of exploratory courses encountered by the student would be quite large, even though they might not have numerous exploratory courses in one given school term.

Home economics and industrial arts seem to be offered in comparable degrees across all organizational types, with the exception of self-contained schools. Because self-contained classes are more likely to occur in elementary buildings, specialized facilities for these courses are generally not available. Thus, it is not surprising that few students are enrolled in these courses.

Program and Practices Characteristics
The question of school organization is always of interest to educators and policymakers. Although the actual organizational plan is often controlled by such factors as demographics and changes in community structure, it is important to identify the effects that these organizational variations might have on programs and practices in the school.

35

In this study, we compared the site visitors' ratings on 23 program characteristics or conditions in the sixth grade, using school organizational type as the independent variable. Thus, we are able to examine the comparative presence or absence of specific program practices in each of the school organizational types in the study: teamed (TM), self-contained (SC), departmentalized (DP), and partially teamed (PT). Figure C shows the results of this comparison.

These data yield a number of interesting and useful findings, most of which are quite logical given the strengths and weaknesses of various organizational patterns.

Ironically, the self-contained classroom was the least likely to have a teacher-adviser or home-based guidance program. Nearly half the observers (46 percent) saw little evidence of such a program in this setting. Team and departmentalized schools were most likely to have these kinds of guidance programs; nearly 77 percent of observers saw some or ample evidence in the teamed schools, 71 percent saw it in departmentalized schools. Why would such programs be rare in self-contained schools? Perhaps it is because the teacher, who is responsible for teaching all subjects, feels the press of time and is not likely to set aside time for an advisory program but does much "guidance" informally during the several hours he or she is with the students. In other settings, such time must be scheduled into the school day in order to ensure that it receives at least some attention from teachers assigned to work as home-base or advisory teachers.

As expected, self-contained schools, since they are primarily elementary schools, tend to have fewer professional counselors available to the children. Only 26 percent of the observers saw ample evidence of such services in these schools, while teamed schools were rated as ample by 71 percent of the observers, departmentalized schools at 61 percent, and partially teamed schools at 51 percent.

Students in teamed schools were much more likely to have opportunities to participate in interest-centered activities in class. Over 57 percent of the raters found ample evidence of such participation in teamed schools. In self-contained schools the ratings were 29 percent, in departmentalized settings 22 percent, and in partially teamed arrangements 32 percent. Teamed and departmentalized schools tended to have more clubs and related organizations in which all students might participate (50 percent had ample evidence in each setting), while self-contained schools provided the fewest opportunities (21 percent rated "ample").

Instructional practices showed variations as well. Departmentalized settings were most likely to use a variety of print and non-print media (78 percent rated ample), while self-contained classrooms (42 percent) and partially teamed classes (54 percent) were least likely to do so. Teamed classes were rated at 57 percent on this variable. Further, teachers are slightly more likely to use diagnostic information about students in departmentalized settings and teamed settings, and somewhat less likely to use it in self-contained and partially teamed schools.

Children are most likely to experience a variety of teaching methods in a departmentalized setting. This is logical since a greater number of different teachers work with them. Little variation exists among the other three types of schools in this regard, since self-contained classes are taught by one person and,

36

Figure C

Presence or Absence of Selected Middle Level Program
Practices and Conditions, Indicating Percentage of
Raters Who Identified Each Practice

Program Characteristics or Conditions in the Sixth Grade

It is recognized, of course, that while no evidence of a condition may be apparent on one day, such a condition may exist. Respond, however, based on your single day's observation by checking in the appropriate column.

1 = little or no evidence that the condition is present
2 = some evidence that the program condition is present
3 = ample evidence that the program condition is present

		Little 1 %	Some 2 %	Ample 3 %
1. Was there evidence of a teacher-adviser or home-base teacher who had clear guidance responsibilities for individual students?	(TM)	20	20	57
	(SC)	46	20	33
	(DP)	29	24	47
	(PT)	38	29	33
2. Was a professional counselor available to sixth grade students when they needed personal assistance?	(TM)	7	21	71
	(SC)	48	26	26
	(DP)	11	28	61
	(PT)	26	23	51
3. Did the student have an opportunity to participate in some interest-centered activities?	(TM)	0	43	57
	(SC)	25	46	29
	(DP)	17	61	22
	(PT)	27	41	32
4. Were clubs or related organizations in which all students might participate available?	(TM)	29	21	50
	(SC)	63	17	21
	(DP)	11	39	50
	(PT)	47	23	30
5. Were varied print and non-print media readily available and used?	(TM)	21	21	57
	(SC)	21	38	42
	(DP)	6	17	78
	(PT)	8	38	54
6. Did teachers seem to use appropriate diagnostic information about student developmental characteristics, learning styles, and skill levels?	(TM)	21	43	36
	(SC)	17	58	25
	(DP)	17	39	44
	(PT)	16	55	29
7. Did teachers use a variety of methods and approaches?	(TM)	21	36	43
	(SC)	21	38	42
	(DP)	11	33	56
	(PT)	11	47	42
8. Was instruction in various aspects of physical growth, including sexual development, provided?	(TM)	36	21	43
	(SC)	71	17	13
	(DP)	65	12	24
	(PT)	57	31	11

		Little 1 %	Some 2 %	Ample 3 %
9. Was information in the areas of sex, alcohol and drugs, and related health concerns provided under appropriate adult leadership?	(TM)	29	29	43
	(SC)	50	33	17
	(DP)	47	18	35
	(PT)	56	29	17
10. Did the student receive instruction in one or more of the basic exploratory areas of art, music, industrial arts, and homemaking?	(TM)	7	14	79
	(SC)	38	25	38
	(DP)	6	22	72
	(PT)	21	17	22
11. Did the student participate in instructional groups of various sizes (full class, small group, pairs, large group)?	(TM)	14	21	64
	(SC)	17	28	67
	(DP)	16	17	50
	(PT)	23	33	49
12. Did the student participate in instructional groups of different types (homogeneous, heterogeneous, interest centered)?	(TM)	0	43	57
	(SC)	29	25	46
	(DP)	12	35	53
	(PT)	20	39	41
13. Did the day include any experiences that addressed the personal-social needs of students?	(TM)	21	29	50
	(SC)	44	39	17
	(DP)	22	28	50
	(PT)	37	31	32
14. Did the student receive direct instruction in skill areas such as reading or writing?	(TM)	7	7	86
	(SC)	25	8	67
	(DP)	11	22	67
	(PT)	7	15	78
15. Were separate subjects correlated or fused in instruction?	(TM)	39	46	15
	(SC)	33	42	25
	(DP)	41	35	24
	(PT)	31	49	19
16. Was the subject matter studied related to "here and now," to the present lives of students?	(TM)	29	50	21
	(SC)	29	50	21
	(DP)	17	39	44
	(PT)	16	40	44
17. Did the physical education activities recognize and accommodate the varied levels of development?	(TM)	31	23	46
	(SC)	50	25	25
	(DP)	44	25	31
	(PT)	27	37	36
18. Did the student participate in an intramural activity?	(TM)	83	8	8
	(SC)	70	13	17
	(DP)	63	13	25
	(PT)	74	14	11
19. Was the community utilized as a resource, either by a resource person, field trip, or related activity?	(TM)	46	31	23
	(SC)	70	17	20
	(DP)	56	22	9
	(PT)	62	22	22

			Little 1 %	Some 2 %	Ample 3 %
20. Was the student recognized individually (a) (addressed directly by name) by (a) at least one teacher during the day?	(a)	(TM)	13	47	40
		(SC)	10	0	90
		(DP)	8	8	85
		(PT)	3	10	87
(b) three or more teachers?	(b)	(TM)	7	40	53
		(SC)	8	25	66
		(DP)	11	0	89
		(PT)	6	3	80
21. Did student-teacher planning occur during the day, or was student input sought on any phase of school operations?		(TM)	57	29	14
		(SC)	55	27	18
		(DP)	53	24	24
		(PT)	56	32	12
22. Was the student involved in situations calling for value discrimination, critical thinking, or analysis of options?		(TM)	21	43	36
		(SC)	33	33	33
		(DP)	41	35	24
		(PT)	31	41	28
23. Did the day include any opportunity for interaction with students of other grade levels?		(TM)	64	14	21
		(SC)	50	21	29
		(DP)	39	22	39
		(PT)	61	18	21

therefore, great variation is not likely, and in the other arrangements, cooperative planning may serve to homogenize teaching styles somewhat. Considering the ratings given in the "some" and "ample" evidence categories, it appears that virtually all students in all settings experience at least some variety in teaching approaches throughout the school day.

Teamed schools are more apt than any other to provide instruction in some aspects of physical growth, including sexual development. The other schools were, in fact, quite *unlikely* to provide such instruction. Similarly, alcohol, drug, and sex-related health information was more common in teamed arrangements than in any others, where the probability of a student encountering such instruction was low, indeed.

Students in teamed schools, departmentalized, or partially teamed schools will probably have direct instruction in exploratory areas, such as music, art, industrial arts, and homemaking; self-contained students are not likely to receive such instruction if specialized facilities (such as shops and home economics labs) are required. They are, however, slightly more likely to take music or art than other students.

Student grouping is variable as well. There is strong evidence that all school types use different size groups, although departmentalized and partially teamed schools are slightly less likely to do so. In addition, most students will have the opportunity to work in groups of different kinds, such as homogeneous by ability, heterogeneous ability, interest, and self-selected. Grouping aside, students in teamed and departmentalized settings are provided with more experiences that address their social-personal needs than students in either self-contained schools or partially teamed schools.

Virtually all students received direct instruction in skill areas, such as reading and writing. Ironically, though, the group slightly less likely to receive such instruction was the self-contained schools. Normally, self-contained arrangements are associated with very strong attention to basic skill instruction. Observers and analysts' judgments seemed to confirm this, although the checklist data didn't.

It can be argued that the teamed schools fail to achieve one of their major goals: the integration of subject matter. According to the observers, only 15 percent saw ample evidence that subjects were being fused or correlated, another 46 percent saw some evidence. Among other school types, the ratings were actually higher in all cases. In addition, both the teamed and self-contained schools received low ratings on whether the subject matter being studied was related to the real world and present lives of students. Both departmentalized and partially teamed arrangements fared somewhat better than teams in this regard.

Students in teamed and partially teamed settings were slightly more likely to be offered a physical education program that was designed to accommodate their developmental needs. However, none of the groups were very apt to participate in an intramural program. The range of ratings in the "little evidence" of participation category was from 63 percent to 83 percent for all schools.

All sixth graders except for those in self-contained classes were about equally likely to use the community as a resource for instruction, although the practice is still not in common use.

Students in teamed classes were somewhat less likely than students in other plans to be individually recognized by a teacher once during the day, or by more than three teachers on shadow study day. Students in partially teamed groups fared the best, overall, in terms of teacher recognition, followed by students in departmentalized and self-contained settings.

Student-teacher planning is uncommon in all settings included in this study. Furthermore, only about a third of the self-contained and teamed schools showed ample evidence of student involvement in situations calling for critical thinking, analysis, or value discrimination, and only a quarter of the students in departmentalized and partially teamed schools had such experiences. Departmentalized schools, however, were more likely to allow sixth graders to mix with students from other grade levels than schools with other instructional organizations.

Conclusions

Based on these analyses, a number of conclusions can be drawn about organizational effects on school programs.

First, the curriculum provided by the middle level school, or schools with teamed or partially-teamed organizations, tend to offer more exploratory opportunities for students than do elementary organizations. Furthermore, these schools make more substantial efforts to deal, in their programs, with issues confronting today's youth: sex, alcohol, drugs, social-emotional development, and personal adjustment.

The content of the curriculum is fairly standard, except for the exploratory component noted above. However, instruction in science is more common in schools other than those with elementary organizations. Because of the specialized nature of this instruction, teachers in self-contained classrooms appear less likely to engage in it than a subject specialist in science working as a member of a team or in an academic department.

Virtually all sixth graders receive some instruction in basic skills, and a surprising number have direct reading instruction sometime during the school day. Physical education is taken by most students, and foreign language is, regrettably, a rarity for sixth graders in America's schools.

The most alarming dimension of sixth grade curriculum is the low incidence of efforts to correlate and integrate the different subjects. The students' day is intellectually fragmented, and they are seldom called upon to utilize learning from one subject in another area. The analysts reached the same conclusion. Most distressing, perhaps, is that interdisciplinary team teaching arrangements actually provided *less* evidence of curriculum correlation than any of the other instructional organizations. One of the most compelling opportunities of teaming is being missed.

Second, instruction is varied at the sixth grade level, and teachers make use of a variety of material. For the most part, grouping is fairly flexible, with most students participating in groups of different types and sizes throughout the school day. Some teachers make use of diagnostic information in preparing their instruction, but the practice is not widespread in this sample. Interest-centered activities were common in team teaching arrangements, and less so in self-contained, departmentalized, and partially teamed settings.

Only rarely does instruction challenge students to critical thinking, value discrimination, or analytic thinking. Much attention is given to the coverage and retention of content; little instruction makes use of higher order intellectual skills. In fact, nearly a third of the observers in this sample saw little or no evidence of such thinking on shadow study day. Instruction, for the most part, is content test driven rather than intellectual skill driven. Cooperative planning between students and teachers is virtually nonexistent.

Finally, the affective climate of the sixth grade is good. Teachers recognize and address students by name, many students received instruction that addressed their personal and social needs, and there were good opportunities for students to participate in a variety of school activities. However, sixth graders tend not to interact with students from other grade levels.

Students in most of the schools have access to good adult advice throughout the day, although teamed and departmentalized programs tend to have more systematic ways of delivering this form of advice. Professional guidance counselors are most often found in middle level schools, and are less common in elementary organizations.

In short, our sixth graders are taught by good people who like students and work hard to provide instructional variety that is interesting for their charges. The curriculum, though, tends not to cultivate higher order intellectual powers, and tends to be highly fragmented. The children have access to adult guidance, and are provided with programs that help them mature as social creatures as well as intellectual ones. The sixth grade, it seems, is generally a pretty nice place to be.

CHAPTER 5

Seven Samples of Reality

During the first celebration of National Middle Level Education Week the nation's educational enterprise went on as usual. All across the United States, nearly a third of our country's population was involved in America's "biggest business" as students, teachers, staff members, board members, or volunteers in our elementary, middle, high schools, and colleges.

The middle of that week, Wednesday, March 11, was a relatively typical day. The Dow Jones Industrial rose 19.97 points as stock prices rebounded. A new poll released that day showed most Americans still viewed President Reagan's explanations of the Iran-Contra affair with skepticism. The Dallas, Tex., paper carried the story of Governor Clement's apology for authorizing cash payments to S.M.U. football players when he was chairman of the board of governors. The Atlanta *Constitution* reported on the federal judge who banned 45 textbooks in Alabama because they espoused, presumably, secular humanism. Another story dealt with the increased failure rate in metro Atlanta schools due to the recently mandated minimum passing score of 70.

For more than 130 sixth grade students in 45 states, however, something special was occurring quietly. They were being "shadowed" as they moved through their regular school day. Their activities were being recorded to provide a look at life in the sixth grade.

This chapter is composed of a sample of seven of the studies made that day. While identifying labels have been removed, they are presented intact. These studies were selected because they were revealing, perceptive, and generally representative. They are not, however, a random sample. Two were chosen from among the self-contained group, three from the teamed group, and two from the fully departmentalized group. They are so identified and presented in that order.

As an important supplement to the studies a number of the observers' reactions are included in this chapter. They are presented in the above groups in the same order. The seven studies and the sampling of observer reactions will give readers a real feel for the data and possibly invite them to draw their own generalizations and conclusions.

Shadow Study Number 1

A six grade elementary school in a large city. Self-contained with limited exception.

Time	Specific behavior at 5-7 minute intervals	Environment	Impression-Comments
7:50	Went to combination locker outside room (organized and neat). Came into room, put books in rack underneath desk. Worked on two worksheets standing up. Everyone sharpened pencil. R. had mechanical pencil.	6 rows of chairs—each desk spaced one desk apart.	
8:00	Bell rang—everyone sat down —said Pledge of Allegiance— sat eyes front (notebook behind his back).	Principal came in and asked teacher to see counselor during P.E.	
8:06	Sitting quietly as teacher continued to pick up work from other students who had not turned in their work.		
8:08	Got book out and began to read—silent reading for class. Teacher passed out paper—going too fast "so you can walk around."	22 students in the class (one girl worked on chart in front desk)	
8:11	Put books away—teacher asked students to get things in order—to go to Spanish.		
8:15	Teacher started Spanish class—R. sat in chair.	Chairs for little children.	
8:17	Students passed out notebooks to R.	Teacher pretty with long fingernails.	
8:19	Raised his hand— Spanish teacher hasn't said class has begun or the date— another student in Spanish said it. R. chewed on end of his pen—twisted the end. Raised his hand—called out answers.	Students graded notebook. Teacher gave lesson totally in Spanish.	Students seemed to understand.
8:29	Continued to listen and grade papers—and chew end of pen— succeeded, threw the end into the trash— began to play with the tip on the end of the paper—tried to take off top of pen.	Teacher shook her head, answered questions in Spanish. Students read answers in Spanish.	Everyone seemed to understand what was happening.

43

Time	Specific behavior at 5-7 minute intervals	Environment	Impression-Comments
8:35	Continued to listen—grade paper—raised hand.		
8:38	Read answer of paper—to check if they were right.		
8:40	Asked another question—put his feet up on desk.		
8:44	Sat as notebooks were collected. Went up front to put papers up. Compared watch with other students.		
8:46	Walked around room—got an encyclopedia. Stood with three other boys to look in encyclopedia.	Students got magazines.	
8:51	Went to talk to another student on the other side of the room. Asked to sit down by teacher—said I asked you if I could talk to him. Sat down behind student and continued talking.	3 boys sat by teacher. Rest of students read or looked at magazines.	
8:54	Still talking to boy in front of him.		10 minutes wasted time—however, did visit with other boys.
8:57	Walked back to regular classroom Asked everyone to be quiet—"Shush you guys!" Got notebooks out— and notes out for Social Studies.		
9:02	Listened to answers—Check up—Answered questions.		Teacher called on students.
9:06	Looked at book and notebook as answers were being reviewed.		
9:12	Continued to listen to lesson.		
9:15	Continued to listen to lesson.		Students all sat and listened and followed along as students read.
9:16	(Questions on Western Europe— Western Germany—corrected) Looked at map as teacher named capital of each Western Europe Country. Look at his watch to see what time it is! Looked at another boy to compare time.		Students all sat and listened and followed along as students read.

44

Time	Specific behavior at 5-7 minute intervals	Environment	Impression-Comments
9:21	Looked through notebook to find page to put notes on.		
9:31	Continued to listen.		
9:32	Teacher assigned 172 review, do check-up 175. Pass forward workbook page.		When R. put his notebook and books away he lined everything up.
9:36	Assigned workbook page— R. started his work. Read question and then would look for answers. Put heading on paper.	Everyone sat quietly and did Social Studies work.	
9:41	Books away—time to go to P.E.		
9:44	Walked down hall—went to gym—coach separated. R. started, made score—got another basket.		Seemed to direct the game.
9:52	Played game—screamed at teammates.		
9:56	Got another basket.		
9:58	Continued to play.		Students seemed to have fun.
9:59	New instructions for double play at free throw line given by coach.		Baseball/Basketball
10:03	Continued playing game.		R. seemed to be very competitive, kept team in charge—was disappointed when his team didn't score
10:09	Continued playing game.		
10:17	Continued to play.		Students seemed to have fun.
10:19	Coach stopped play. Teacher rules—went over.		
10:22	Lines up on black line.		
10:26	Walked back to class— Graded papers were on desk. Looked through them— Sorted them out and put them in a folder.		Class was very quiet— waited for teacher to return.

Time	Specific behavior at 5-7 minute intervals	Environment	Impression-Comments
10:29	Finished putting papers away. Turned to social studies work and began to do homework.		Everyone was on task.
10:32	Teacher came in and asked students to get math out. R. continued with social studies work. Put it away in folder and got math workbook out. Asked to pass up pp. 207-209, homework. R. looked surprised—Schedule was not on board—		
10:39	Waited at desk while teacher collected assignment.		Frustrated, then realized that he had done assignment.
10:40	Listened as teacher went over workbook exercise. Always checked things out. Helped boy next to him read correct answer.	Students who didn't have work sat quietly.	Teacher comment: "Sixth graders can't find paper out of notebook."
10:46		"Tore it out— put it somewhere You know, M."	Class very quiet—asked to be "more quiet"
10:47	Continued checking work assignment.	Teacher comment— "S. you are not paying attention— put your feet flat on the floor."	I am very impressed with R.'s neatness. Everything is in order. His books, papers, pens, everything! He has it together!
10:52	Graded paper as teacher read answer to worksheet. R. claimed he hadn't graded. Made comment to S.—"This is corny."		
10:59	Gave answer to p. 44. Teacher read them.		
11:02	Passed papers up front, helped pick up math papers.		
11:06	Sat down—turn to page teacher is talking about— Had math on front board— Math Sets 73 (11-16), 79 (25-30), 82(23-30)		
11:09	Teacher gave assignment. R. began to work on assignment.		All students started doing work.

46

Time	Specific behavior at 5-7 minute intervals	Environment	Impression-Comments
11:10	Walked up to teacher and asked about how to work it—Teacher helped R. with problem.	Teacher—said "Go back to where you did it."	
11:18	R. continued to do his math work.		
11:24	Continued to do his math work.	Teacher read Teacher's Manual to get ready for next subject (Science).	Several students sat doing nothing—paper and book in front of them—not knowing what to do.
11:29	Looked over his math assignment. Put book away underneath desk—Put paper in notebook. Got up and asked Teacher about social studies worksheet. R. continued with lines on worksheet for Social Studies.	Teacher moved J. to front.	
11:35	Teacher asked students to get Science Books out. R. continued to color chart. Asked to get a clean piece of paper out—R. still.	Teacher—write your Mom a note that you need paper.	
11:38	Got book out and turned to the correct page. Put words read out on little notepad.	S. went back to her desk.	
11:43	Continued writing words (20). Read pp. 196-200. Put words in alphabetical order and define words. Sat and watched teacher talk to M. Got up and gave M. his words.	M. sent out of room. S. had to go back to the front seat Students sat and read and started defining words.	
11:50	Started to put them in alphabetical order—put up in alphabetical order.		
11:56	Continued working on definitions; got up and asked teacher question—got a computer dictionary from teacher.	Teacher stood in front of room and graded papers.	
12:07	R. still working on definitions; students started washing their hands for lunch		

Time	Specific behavior at 5-7 minute intervals	Environment	Impression-Comments
12:10	Washing their hands—left papers on desk—got in line to go to lunch.		
12:19	Got a hamburger and fries. Sat down with the rest of the boys.		
12:29	Finished lunch— Went to the water fountain.		
12:31	Asked to go out (if finished).		
12:39	Playing basketball with a group of students.		P. E. coaches lend students basketballs.
12:45	Whistle blew—students stood in line in front of the door.		It felt very good to be able to go outside.
12:50	Stood at door until teacher came to get them.		
12:52	Got his reading book out.		
12:56	R. got his book out and turned to page II and started reading.	Moved S. again by J. Students sat and read.	
12:57		Teacher walked around and checked that students were reading. Could hear projector from room next to class—very distracting.	
1:05	R. still reading his book.		
1:12	R. still reading his book.		
1:13	Stopped reading—started to thumb through his book—bent back and moved his neck around.		
1:14	Went back to reading.		
1:20	Teacher passed out worksheet—R. got one.		
1:22	Put heading on white page—started working on worksheet.		
1:26	Finished first worksheet.		
1:30	Started on worksheet 2—turned in first blue page.		
1:34	Finished worksheet—started working on science homework (definitions).	Teacher collected other blue worksheet. Took up answers to blue worksheet. Teacher told students to get English books.	

48

Time	Specific behavior at 5-7 minute intervals	Environment	Impression-Comments
1:40	Still working on science words.	Teacher asked if they would get English books.	R. felt it was okay to continue to work because it will take the teacher a while to get started.
1:42	Teacher made a comment that students could do better—today do better—R. said his grade wasn't bad. Started working on assignment page 83—in English book.	Present time—But everyone knows what that means—Everyone understands.	
1:45	Had students take a restroom break. Came back and started working.		
1:55	R. continued to work on chapter questions in English book.		
2:00	Continued working on English—finished—Got his Science book out to continue with his definitions.		
2:06	Continued working on definitions.		Very on task and deliberate about assignments.
2:07	Finished—sighed real loud—put his head down on desk— stretched out. Students left for Band and then lined up for fine arts.	Teacher made decision about math work.	
2:15	Started fine arts. R. sat and watched a student cheat.		
2:16	R. watched, smiled.		
2:21	We are not finished. Students volunteered to sing song.		
2:34	Continued watching commercials. R. sat and talked to M. while commercial was on.		
2:35	Took R. to interview.		

End-of-Day Interview

1. Assume that a new kid moved next door and would be your schoolmate. What are three good things about this school that you would tell him/her?

    (a) No gangs— no rockers—no one to pick on us

    (b) It's clean

    (c) New equipment for P.E.

2. *What are three things about this school that you would change, if you could?*

   (a) Go outside more often
   (b) Longer lunch periods
   (c) More breaks—restroom
   (d) Not having a lot of work

3. *How do you feel, in general, about your teachers?*

   She's nice, strict "a little"—Gets on our back.
   All nice, Fine Arts and P.E. the most fun.
   Spanish teacher is the meanest.

4. *Is there a person in this school that you would readily turn to for help on a personal problem?*

   "A friend"

5. *How do you feel about the way students treat one another?*

   Most of them treat them okay—they're nice except the ones in special classes—they get in fights.

6. *How do you feel, in general, about your classes? Do they challenge you?*

   It's a lot of work and too little time to do it!
   Yes—most of class challenges us—Do a lot of reading and research.

7. *Do you have opportunities to help make decisions about what goes on in class?*

   Sometimes, But she doesn't listen—"You don't run the class—I do"—What the teacher says.

Shadow Study Number 2

A K-6 elementary school with self-contained sixth grade

Time	Specific behavior at 5-7 minute intervals	Environment	Impression-Comments
8:45	Following a short welcome from the instructor the Star Spangled Banner is played and G. stands with all other students with hand over heart and looking at a small flag in the classroom, pledges allegiance to the flag and then sits down.	The teacher enters smiling—The class room appears large enough for the 31 students. Colorful and interesting posters and lettering are round the walls above the blackboards. There are papers on each desk with squares on them and periodically the instructor will announce: "Table three give yourselves a square because your table is clear" or "Mary, give yourself a square because you are very attentive"etc.	The teacher called all of his students very special. Said he had been in another city giving a lecture all about his wonderful kids. One lady wants to come out and see them. He really missed all of them. Students would interact and chat, but in soft undertones. A student came in late making a loud comment as to it being a bad day. The teacher, without

Time	Specific behavior at 5-7 minute intervals	Environment	Impression-Comments
8:55	The student turned in some paper he had been working on since he sat down. He made some quiet comment to a girl across from him, put his glasses in a case, opened a book in his desk and began reading in a semi-slouch position.	The teacher embraced students freely--boys and girls alike. Love was obviously present!	raising his voice, asked her to come in quietly again as she should not draw attention to herself being tardy. The student did so and the teacher put his arms around her and had her sit down.
9:00	Teacher announced that as they completed their journal they would go to the cafeteria for song practice. (It must have been his journal he handed in for he rose and went from the room with his classmates.) G. was wearing a white tee shirt and bright colored shorts—as were most of the boys.		
9:10	G. did not balk at directions to line up on the stage. He knew the words to all the songs and participated with vigor. Some of the boys around him would jiggle and dance to the music when the teacher was not looking, but G. did not.	The cafeteria was clean and the students stood on three levels of stairs to sing.	The music for their singing was on tape and was electric type accompaniment and the student sang along with gusto! They were patriotic songs. Good beat! The instructor would address the group as ladies and gentlemen. "I appreciate your giving me your attention."
9:20	When the students were allowed to sit down or walk out and come in again a little faster each time, G. would cooperate. There were very few who acted up.	At one point, the teacher said to one "You are excused! You are not being polite to me! You are excused right now!' (She quietly left.)	As rearranging was going on, the girls were ready first. The teacher led in the applause for them.
9:30	Students went outside to enter the classroom in order not to disturb other classes. G. wiggled a bit, but not in a disruptive way.		At one point one of the students made a suggestion the teacher accepted and all gave the boy applause!
9:45	He was ready to be a "secret agent."	Instructor said, "They don't come any better than you! No one comes better than you."	The teacher told all of the students who did not "blurtout" to give themselves 3 squares.

Time	Specific behavior at 5-7 minute intervals	Environment	Impression-Comments
9:55	G. put his glasses on to read and write.		Teacher spoke in Spanish to two students who just the month before came from Peru.
10:00	Student does not offer suggestions or raise his hand often.	Teacher said, "I'm so proud of sixth-graders who work so hard, man, I love you, give yourselves another square."	The instructor had the students try to decipher his "special" code. When they did, it said, "Mr. A loves you. "
10:20	G. picked up a paper by his desk and put it in the wastebasket. He laughed at some humorous remark of a student.	For listening carefully give yourselves another square. I love my task workers."	
10:25	Students exchanged their own codes.		
10:30 to 11:00	Students first went to the gym and then outside for basketball. G. cooperated with the other students, taking his turn at hitting at the hoop and chasing his own ball. Also, he did make a basket every now and then. He obviously enjoyed the activity.		
11:00 to 12:00	G. went with the other students outside again, but this time it was to work with a television program on bus safety. He obviously was interested in what was going on. As things began to drag a little while the TV men were working around, the students started playing tag and running around.	It was a truly gorgeous spring day outside.	The TV people wasted some time by not making good decisions fast enough.
12:00 to 1:00	Lunch		
1:00	G. was quite pleased when his mother arrived to help along with four others. The mothers were in another room doing something toward decorating		The mothers were very warmly greeted by the instructor, and they in turn seemed delighted to be there.

Time	Specific behavior at 5-7 minute intervals	Environment	Impression-Comments
	the mothers' day books the students had made.		
1:10	Reading time for the teacher to read aloud to the class. G. listened, but seemed to be interested in impressing a girl across from him just how much he could twist his fingers and arms.		
1:40	Students wrote poems for their mother on construction paper to be used as a card to go with the little book. G. entered in and seemed quite pleased with his card.	The helping mothers were to check the spelling. It was obvious, as G.'s mom hugged him, they were on good terms. Students handed their cards to the teacher as they left the classroom to go to play their instruments.	
1:45	Students assembled in a small classroom where orchestra was being taught. G. played the cello with confidence. The orchestra instructor mentioned that G. played perfectly and had a very good ear.		The orchestra room was the science room. There was no room for a piano.
2:35	I made myself aware to G. and the instructor excused us both for the interview.		

End-of-Day Interview

1. Assume that a new kid moved next door and would be your schoolmate. What are three good things about this school that you would tell him/her?

    (a) The school has a lot of nice people

    (b) Teachers are really great

    (c) You can rely on almost anyone you choose for help

2. What are three things about this school that you would change, if you could?

    (a) I would like the whole thing to be newer.

    (b) I would like nicer facilities.

    (c) Better play-ground equipment.

3. How do you feel, in general, about your teachers?

    They are just great.

4. *Is there a person in this school that you would readily turn to for help on a personal problem?*
   L.G.—a friend. (he offered this without hesitation)

5. *How do you feel about the way students treat one another?*
   Well, I have only been here a couple of months, but I think, just fine.

6. *How do you feel, in general, about your classes? Do they challenge you?*
   Yes, they challenge me. They are fine. I can handle it.

7. *Do you have opportunities to help make decisions about what goes on in class?*
   Once in a while.

Shadow Study Number 3

A 6-8 middle school with teaming

Time	Specific behavior at 5-7 minute intervals	Environment	Impression-Comments
9:00	Sits attentively at desk when bell rings and PA announcements made. Listens well as does rest of class.	Advisor/Advisee Program	Principal praises students for good behavior over PA but reminds them that wearing shorts (normally not allowed) is not a mandate for too much freedom or relaxation of rules.
9:07	Continues sitting at desk paying attention to class-room routine, i.e., Lunch Count, etc.	Student dressed in red tee shirt and white shorts ready for special Intra-mural Program in honor of National Middle School Education Week.	Group of 5 students read essays on "Why I Like My Middle School"
9:12	Laughs and smiles contin-uously while watching two students play eraser tag. Doesn't volunteer to participate when eraser falls off heads of players as others in class do.		Principal praises stu-dents for attendance at last night's 8th grade program, students going to high school next year.
9:17	Continues sitting quietly, enjoying game activity and makes comment to fellow student sitting next to her about what's going on.		Students *all* very orderly but relaxed,when playing game. When game gets too noisy (10 minutes later) classroom student leader and teacher stop game, re-group and play another—7-Up, which is quiet game format.

Time	Specific behavior at 5-7 minute intervals	Environment	Impression-Comments
9:22	Volunteers to play new 7-Up game by raising hand but not chosen as one of five players.		
9:27	Puts head down on desk with thumb up according to rules of game and is secretly touched by one of players.		
9:33	Sits quietly at desk waiting for class to begin. Gets out math book and homework as directed by substitute teacher.	Math class with substitute teacher. Class noisy entering room but quiets down when class begins. Math papers displayed on big bulletin board that says: Learning Math—Having A Great Time.	Students fairly attentive in spite of inadequate leadership by substitute. Things slowly deteriorate as teacher fumbles for a plan of action during this class. Students help him out by saying it's time to correct last night's homework, which helps situation for a few minutes. Kids politely "do own thing" at seats while teacher engages a handful of kids in correcting homework. Most not on task.
9:38	Sits in front row seat quietly listening/watching teacher review units of measure with total class. Doesn't raise hand to respond to teacher review questions.	Classroom bright with big windows along two sides of room. Bulletin boards (except for student work section) look faded and worn. Displaying posters and announcements.	
9:45	Raises hand and volunteers to answer measurement question stated incorrectly by girl who sits behind her.		Class now quite noisy and off task due to either disinterest in subject of adding minutes/seconds and/or monotone delivery of information by substitute. Observe some horseplay, some social talking, some reading non-math books, and some working on math problems. About 10 people trying to interact positively with substitute teacher.
9:51	Raises hand to answer question about addition of mixed fractions but ignored by teacher who states "people in back of room should respond to questions for a change."		
9:56	Sits quietly and raises hand to answer question about addition of minutes and seconds, but not called on.		
10:02	Sits at desk quietly with head resting on hand and patiently watching and listening to substitue teacher's questions and explanations.		

Time	Specific behavior at 5-7 minute intervals	Environment	Impression-Comments
10:08	Passes back new homework paper and pauses to ask substitute teacher a brief question.		
10:14	Smiles at joke of teacher and packs up things to move on to next class.		
10:19	Stands in circle around teacher politely waiting for directions from teacher on what to do.	Outdoor Science Class—teacher assembles class outside classroom to do planting/raking activity on school grounds.	Students now becoming curious about my activities and whether I'm going to follow their class all day. Very inquisitive, but polite in their questions.
10:25	Watches teacher who demonstrates how to use rake correctly to prepare ground for planting. Takes rake and imitates teacher.	Assigns allergic students to be record keepers and rest of class into two subgroups for ground preparation tasks.	Students actively and physically involved in pruning, weeding, raking, digging, and plowing sections of school grounds.
10:31	Pulls weeds by hand after giving up rake to another classmate. Keeps on task without allowing self to be too distracted by occasional horseplay by classmates.		
10:37	Assists teacher with pulling of weeds by hand and keeps self busy on task.	Older special education student comes by and distracts a student.	Teacher circulates among group of students to provide direction.
10:42	Pauses briefly to smile and talk to two girls also pulling weeds by hand, moves to another location.	Teacher quickly redirects his behavior away from class. Record keepers (students) circulate to keep track of and record names of students who (1) mess around and (2) are hard workers.	Teacher tells students to wash hands for lunch.
10:47	Walks to cafeteria with class, selects table/seat and sits down alone to work on homework, while two friends go to buy milk.	Cafeteria with assigned tables for teams.	Students in cafeteria appear happy and active. Noisy but not unruly. Only direct supervision for approximately 250 kids is circulating Dean, a parent volunteer, and an aide.

56

Time	Specific behavior at 5-7 minute intervals	Environment	Impression-Comments
10:53	Talks with three friends but works on homework at same time. Eats no lunch but sips glass of juice.		
10:59	Continues sitting at lunch table listening to chatter of friends. Doesn't appear to be actively talking, but more a respectful listener.		
11:14	Walks out of cafeteria to continuation of science class without fanfare or conversation with others.		
11:20	Sits at assigned seat and quietly listens to teacher lecture on light rays.	Second half of Science class	Student under observation is very business-like in school. Takes it very seriously and programs herself accordingly. Tends to be a well-prepared, less social student than most in her class.
11:26	Watches 3 fellow students do simulated "light walk" activity with some interest. Responds accurately and succinctly to light beam questions asked of her unexpectedly by teacher.	Students back in the classroom (instead of outdoors) for this half. Classroom bright, colorful, cheerful and full of hands-on science models and materials. Bulletin boards full of student work (groups), charts, posters, and information sheets. Posters of science on walls.	
11:33	Raises hand to answer question of teacher but not called upon to respond.		
11:40	Walks to locker with rest of class to get ready for p.m. classes. Walks out talking and smiling with a boy classmate.		
11:45	Returns to class, sits promptly down in seat, opens book to correct pages, and begins copying story from printed text. Intramural Sports	Reading class is shortened today by 30 minutes because of special Intramural Sports Competition scheduled from 12:00	A student of the class informs me that they have to spend their time this period copying story word-for-word from reading textbook

Time	Specific behavior at 5-7 minute intervals	Environment	Impression-Comments
		to 1:20 this afternoon.	because they were "bad" in class yesterday.
11:52	Continues copying text with no interruption of activity.		
11:57	Talks to teacher briefly as he makes informal comment to her.		This room is same as math class this a.m. so has same substitute teacher in charge. Class works silently at seats copying story in best handwriting.
12:02	Walks from Reading Class to gymnasium with two girlfriends.	Gymnasium— Intramural Competition PE teachers have organized series of intramural activities for team competition, i.e., shoot "birdie" into coffee can basket from distance of 10 feet.	Student under observation is very predictable in behavior. Always seems to be in right place, at right time, doing right thing. Student appears more subdued, mature, disciplined than most of peers.
12:13	Shoots basket in intramural competition for team but misses. Shakes head in frustration when misses.		
12:20	Sits on bleacher with rest of teammates watching competition of other sixth graders in action. Is a quiet, patient observer.		All 120 students appear to be enjoying the variety and simplicity of the intramural game activities in their own way. Lots of laughter, peer support, and noisy cheers evident. All appear to follow rules consistently —rules for behavior, game playing, bathroom needs, etc.
12:26	Runs to assigned spot on gym floor with rest of team and gets in back of line. Doesn't hurry or push way to front of line as others in group appear to.		
12:32	Carries ball on spoon very carefully in second type of team competition without dropping it in relay.		
12:37	Sits on bleachers with rest of team after contest is over. Chats with girlfriend who moves over to sit next to her.		

Time	Specific behavior at 5-7 minute intervals	Environment	Impression-Comments
12:43	Watches demonstration of another competitive game of pushing ball with paddle using two hands. Pays attention without asking questions or laughing aloud at demonstration. Smiles to self.		
12:55	Plays seat-swapping game on bleachers informally with 3 girls while awaiting her team's turn to play ball/paddle game.		
1:00	Takes turn hitting ball with paddle and does well in terms of speed and accuracy. Sits down against wall as soon as finishes.		
1:06	Looks around bleachers and talks to peers sitting on bleachers behind her.		
1:12	Stands in line talking to girl behind her, waiting for turn in relay of putting on pants/shirt over clothes, running to marker, and taking clothes off upon return.		
1:18	Laughs at antics of boy teammate who makes a fool of himself losing pants in relay race.		
1:25	Walks from cafeteria to continuation of Reading Class. Discusses Intramural games with a friend.	Continuation of Reading Class after interruption of Intramural Program (in math classroom facility of this a.m.)	
1:31	Reads book silently to self as part of Silent Sustained Reading Program of school.		
1:37	Continues reading book in silence. Appears absorbed in content.		
1:43	Packs up books to move to next period class which is English.		
1:50	Listens to teacher discuss plans for today's English Class. Smiles when teacher compliments her and others on their recent storing writing efforts.	English Class held in same classroom facility as Advisor—Advisee class this a.m.	Teacher soft-spoken in delivery and students very quiet and attentive as she talks about content of their literature papers.
1:57	Works on math homework in subtle manner as		Teacher's name is Irish and she spends consider-

59

Time	Specific behavior at 5-7 minute intervals	Environment	Impression-Comments
	teacher reads excerpts from literature papers written by students.		able time talking about St. Patrick's Day and Irish customs. Instructs students to begin thinking about ideas for writing Leprechaun story. She plays Irish music to set mood.
2:03	Listens to classmate who chooses to read paper written by student under observation in sharing session.		Student under observation is very task-oriented as she immediately acts on any suggestion made, i.e., redo cover for literature paper or jot down ideas for Leprechaun story.
2:08	Reads aloud from literature textbook when called upon by teacher to do so.		
2:13	Reads silently to self as teacher instructs students to finish story on own. Teacher walks by, notices math homework on desk and asks her to put it away which she does.		
2:20	Colors cover for literature paper she wrote earlier in week because teacher tells her it could be neater and better.		
2:27	Writes down ideas for Leprechaun story.		
2:32	Sits down at assigned table to listen to mini-lecture on Feudalism and Mannerism as it relates to today's assignment.	Social Studies Class Room is bright with lots of windows, work stations, lots of student work on bulletin boards, and lots of writing on blackboard with input and notes for students to copy and learn.	Desks rearranged by teacher (before students entered classroom) from straight rows to small groups of 4. Purpose is to facilitate project work—diagram a manor. Teacher indicates this project will receive a group grade.
2:38	Turns in original Code of Armor to teacher upon request to do so.		
2:45	Works on group project which is to diagram a manor complete with castle, church, village,		

Time	Specific behavior at 5-7 minute intervals	Environment	Impression-Comments
	fields, etc. Smiles and interacts with 3 people in her small group cluster.		
2:52	Reads aloud from social studies textbook at teacher's request—an activity which goes on simultaneously with diagram/project work.		
2:55	Interview with student as must board bus at 3:15.		

End-of-Day Interview

1. Assume that a new kid moved next door and would be your schoolmate. What are three good things about this school that you would tell him/her?

Teachers are nice
Everybody—kids and teachers—try to help you
Parents are involved in school activities

2. What are three things about this school that you would change, if you could?

Not much except food in cafeteria. Today I forgot my lunch as I usually bring it from home.

3. How do you feel, in general, about your teachers?

Like them a lot. They always give me lots of help when I need it— individually. Very anxious to please students. They truly care about kids.

4. Is there a person in this school that you would readily turn to for help on a personal problem?

Yes, Mrs. _____, my English and Advisor/Advisee teacher.

5. How do you feel about the way students treat one another?

Not very well - because they laugh when you do something wrong. I try to stay away from them and keep to myself to avoid this situation.

6. How do you feel, in general, about your classes? Do they challenge you?

Yes, for the most part. Science and social studies take most work. Also, I learn most in those classes.

7. Do you have opportunities to help make decisions about what goes on in class?

There are times when we get to choose what we want to do for a special project, but not very often. I would like more opportunities to make choices.

Shadow Study Number 4
A 6-8 middle school with teaming

Time	Specific behavior at 5-7 minute intervals	Environment	Impression-Comments
8:25	B. came right up to me and said "if there's anything I	Very active, a lot of conversation and	The teacher is moving from one

Time	Specific behavior at 5-7 minute intervals	Environment	Impression-Comments
	can do, let me know; we are supposed to help visitors around." He has a very large notebook and 4 textbooks on his desk. He sits in the front seat of the 3rd row.	move—going on. B. is having a difficult time sitting still.	small group to the next. The classroom seems very unorganized and hectic.
8:30	He has calmed down and is tapping on his books. He turns around and gives his "fist" to a boy sitting behind him.	He begins to slap at the boy behind him. The class is still unorganized.	I am wondering how the teacher will ever gain control.
8:35	He is still wiggling in his seat and seems ready for the day to begin.	Very hectic. The teacher begins to give directions concerning an upcoming "crab ball" game. Some students are listening, others appear uninterested.	
8:40	B. is coloring in his notebook with a pencil. He deliberately breaks the pencil lead and requests permission to sharpen his pencil. The bell rings as he's at the pencil sharpener— he quickly gets his books and disappears into the hallway.	The hallway is extremely crowded. Students are pushing and shoving their ways to and from their lockers. He has disappeared out of sight.	The pushing and shoving is very frustrating. Since they are one team on their wing, I would think that classes could be dismissed at different times so the hallway would be more orderly.

Reading—15 students in class

Time	Specific behavior at 5-7 minute intervals	Environment	Impression-Comments
8:45	I found his reading class which he quickly ran to before I could follow him. He is asking about a test grade and how it will affect his final grade. He has his big notebook and only 1 textbook.	Colorful classroom with student work displayed throughout. The class is reviewing a vocabulary test while the teacher gives the correct answer.	Academic and student oriented classroom. Lots of books, materials and student work everywhere. Students seem to like this classroom and the teacher.
8:55	He is leaning his head on his hand and now seems bored. He gets his paper back and received a 98.	The class is still correcting papers. They score the papers and return them to their classmates.	The teacher moves very quickly and does not allow much opportunity for students to correct their errors. Teacher has students tell the class what they made. One student who did not do so well was obviously embarrassed to tell his grade.

Time	Specific behavior at 5-7 minute intervals	Environment	Impression-Comments
9:00	He turns his pages to 475 and yells out the page # for his classmates. He appears to not like choral reading.	The class is assigned individual lines for a choral-reading exercise. Some of the students excited about the assignment; others are not.	
9:05	He is tapping his left foot while he reads in unison with the class. He reads his individual stanzas beautifully—with expression.	The class is paying attention and doing an excellent job.	
9:15	He is reading his stanza again, preparing to be tape-recorded. He then participates in the actual recording of the poem. He does an excellent job.	The teacher is encouraging students to use expression and be creative. She has them move the desks closer together, in a line up front so the recorder will pick up each student's lines.	Students have improved through her encouragement. The class needed to move and she responded to this need by having them rearrange their seating arrangement.
9:25	He is listening to the tape being played back. He has his head hidden in his arms when he is about to listen to himself. The teacher taps him on the head and he looks up laughing. He turns bright red when he hears himself on the recorder.	Most students are really enjoying this activity. They like hearing themselves on the tape.	The teacher asks students to critique the choral reading. Students do a good job in identifying strengths and weaknesses.
9:30	He puts his desk back, organizes his books into a stack, and puts his jacket on.	The students are organizing their materials preparing to leave.	The teacher gives directions about (1) a vocabulary test for Friday (2) A talent show in May and (3) Upcoming career day. Students don't seem to be listening.
9:31	He's dismissed and again took off quickly and I couldn't catch him.		

English—30 students

Time	Specific behavior	Environment	Impression-Comments
9:35	As I walk into the English class he and a girl are pushing each other and being very nasty.	The teacher intervenes and makes him push his desk back toward this girl.	The class seems very crowded. A bulletin board displays the heading "Star Brat of the Week" and has some of the children's pictures underneath the heading. A student explained that it was for her A/A group.
	He is pouting and when his name is called by the teacher taking roll he would not answer.	The teacher stops and says, "Are you here, B.?" He finally answers.	

63

Time	Specific behavior at 5-7 minute intervals	Environment	Impression-Comments
	He is passing his home-work paragraph to the front.		
9:40	His head is resting on his hand and he is still upset over the incident with the girl. He does not take out his English folder when instructed and when he is asked to pass out workbooks he agrees but *takes his time.*	The class is given directions about their workbook pages and are to change papers to correct answers, (They are not allowed to write in their notebooks.)	Teacher seems very bored and not very motivated.
9:45	He is now on task and is correcting a paper. His mood has changed and he seems happier.	The students return the corrected papers.	Teacher has students raise hands to indicate how many they got wrong.
9:55	He has his head in hand and is yawning. He quickly turns to the page and lays on his book.	Teacher gives directions for pg. 305. Students begin to work.	*As students are working* the teacher remains at her podium and gives the following directions (1)what a "folder check" involves. (2) there will be a folder check on Monday, and (3) the crab ball letters needed from parents.
10:02	He gets right to work and appears to *think* about every answer. At one point he stopped and began to tap his pencil and talk to himself.	Students are not listening to the teacher. They finish their assignment very quickly.	Teacher never leaves the podium.
10:07	He is trying to communicate with a friend across the room. Neither one is being successful at lip reading. He puts a grade on his paper and begins to organize his materials and puts his jacket on.	The class is correcting their papers. The teacher gives the correct answers.	The teacher does not explain why the answers are such. She ends by indicating that there will be a worksheet page on prepositional phrases due tomorrow that will count as their daily grade.
10:13	He is ready to go and tapping his pencil. He is also yawning.	Class is ready to go.	There was no instruction. Just one workbook page after another. The class seemed very bored.
10:14	They are dismissed. He disappears out the door but must wait in line at the next class-room.	The hallways are very loud and crowded.	

Time	Specific behavior at 5-7 minute intervals	Environment	Impression-Comments
Math—29 students			
10:17	He immediately takes out his homework to review.	Students appear on tasks and are correcting their homework.	The teacher is quickly discussing decimals and their homework assignment. Some students are not prepared or listening. She then instructs students to pass out workbooks and complete 25 problems.
10:25	He takes out a piece of paper and begins completing the assignment. He finishes in 6 min.	Students finish the assignment in 2-6 min.	Teacher then instructs students to begin their homework assignment written on the board.
10:35	He is working very carefully and slowly on his homework assignment. He stops at one point and mouths something to a friend across the room. He then gets back on task.	Many students have finished their homework. Students do not seem to be studying their vocabulary words. The noise level is increasing.	The teacher tells students that when they finish their homework they are to review their geometry vocabulary words for a test on Friday.
10:47	He finishes his homework and puts it in the basket. He organizes all of his materials and puts his jacket on. (13 minutes left before the period ends.) He jumps up, grabs his friend and they rush to the back of the room. He seems to enjoy the game.	Students are not studying.

The teacher moves them to the front where they play an organized game. | Teacher announces that students can select a math game (no more than 3 per game) and play quietly on the floor. The period seems unorganized and it appears the teacher did not have enough planned. |
10:58	He is still playing even after instructed to put the game away and prepare for dismissal. The teacher disciplines him and he obeys.	Students are in their seats and ready to go.	Teacher reminds students about vocabulary test on Friday.
11:00	He rushes out the door, punches a friend at his locker and runs into his Social Studies class.	Students are still getting organized and the teacher has started taking roll.	The teacher warns students about the "poptest" they will have in a few minutes.
11:13	He is listening attentively and raises his hand when a question is asked. He looks like he enjoys this class. He asks the teacher a question about the time zone.	The class is very attentive while the teacher or a student is talking.	A very academic *and* student oriented classroom. Students' work and names are displayed everywhere.

Time	Specific behavior at 5-7 minute intervals	Environment	Impression-Comments
11:17	He gets out a piece of paper for a "poptest" and numbers 1-10.	Students are trying to get the teacher off task.	The teacher is very organized and has a quick review.
11:26	He is still on task taking the quiz. He asks the teacher if there will be a "challenge" question. He likes to keep *all* of his materials close to him!	The class enjoys this teacher and seem very anxious to do their best.	Students exchange papers again to correct their classmates.
11:33	From the expression he must have done well on his test. He prepares to do the board work and gets right to work.	Students ask if the board work will count as a grade.	Teacher has 10 problems on board for students to complete.
11:45	He gets out his book and skill packet and begins working. He leaves for the restroom (dancing out of the room) and is gone for 2 minutes.	As students are working they are instructed to begin to prepare for lunch.	Teacher is continually talking while students work. He discusses the crab ball game and 4 days for the ITBS testing. Teacher never leaves the front of the room..
11:52	He runs in the door punching the boy in front of him. He gets back to work and when told to line up for lunch he immediately put his pencil down and "lined-up."	Students feel comfortable in this class. The teacher is constantly teasing the students.	The teacher has a good rapport with the students because he seems to genuinely *care* about them.
12:00-12:30 lunch	He is very rowdy. He first goes to one line then another and finally selects the salad bar. He said he didn't like cheeseburgers or pizza. After lunch he ran back to his social studies classroom and organized his materials. He was ready to go.	The class is active and has much energy. Hallways are loud and crowded. Students must return immediately to class.	The teacher seems to let them vent their anxieties because he didn't even discipline students for rolling on the ground or yelling. The class needed 5-10 minutes of "free time" after lunch. They had no time to work off the structured activities.

Science—30 students

Time	Specific behavior at 5-7 minute intervals	Environment	Impression-Comments
12:35	He ran to the front to ask the teacher a question. He seems to have more energy. He is tapping his pencil and gets out of his seat while the teacher is talking—he is reprimanded.	The class is confusing. A substitute teacher is in charge while the regular teacher is on pregnancy leave. Lots of movement, direction unclear, students unruly.	Students are doing anything they can to confuse the teacher. Teacher tells class to 1st—complete test 2nd—answer the discussion question on the board. 3rd—complete a worksheet.

Time	Specific behavior at 5-7 minute intervals	Environment	Impression-Comments
12:45	He is on task and completes the test. He stops, gives a *loud* sigh and continues to work on the discussion question.	Three boys in the back are looking through a wrestling magazine and *never* completed the assignment.	Misspelled word on board—efficiency spelled "effiency."
1:00	He places test in the basket and picks up the next worksheet.	Class is *very* disruptive and loud.	Teacher gives instructions while class works. They can take the worksheet home for homework if they don't finish.
1:10	He is out of his seat and showing a picture to a friend. He returns to seat and pretends his pencil is a gun—he shoots at his classmates and the teacher. He organizes his books and gets his jacket on.		
1:13	He is dismissed. He *runs* to his locker, literally *throws* everything into the locker and runs out the door yelling to the p.e. track.	Again, the hallways are so crowded—students are always pushing. The class ran out to the track.	It was so good to get outside and get fresh air—I could understand why the class was in such a hurry.
1:25	He is jumping up and down, excited about playing softball. He wants to be a captain but is not picked.	The class has broken into small groups and are not paying attention to the student teacher or teacher.	The student teacher informs the class of a written test on Friday covering the rules of softball. No one asks any questions.
1:30	He was the third boy picked and was excited to be on his friend's team. He is standing between 2 girls and continues to tease and poke at both of them.	Class is very active. They seem to be enjoying moving around.	There is not much evidence of team spirit. There is little cheering until the student teacher gets the teams going.
1:37	He is good—hits the ball well and very competitive. When his teammates go up to bat he yells threatening remarks to them.	Everyone seems to be doing their own thing.	
2:00	He bought a Coke and some M&M's which he quickly disposed of. He then ran to his next class with 5 other classmates.	There seemed to be no closure on the game. Students were arguing over who had *won*.	
2:10	He is listening attentively to the art directions on fingerprinting. He is standing perfectly still.	The art room is very unorganized and stark with no students' work displayed. Students are very attentive— afraid to move.	The teacher is condescending and sarcastic to the students. He spends over 5 min. making a big deal over a very insignificant problem.

67

Time	Specific behavior at 5-7 minute intervals	Environment	Impression-Comments
2:15	He still has not moved and is paying close attention to the teacher.	Students seem bored and ready to get to work.	The teacher is telling the students they are impatient and don't follow directions so their projects always fail.
2:20	He gets his card for finger printing and begins to ask his friend what to do.	Very directed with no room for creativity. Stifling environment. Students don't seem to enjoy the activity.	The teacher reprimands 3 students for *all* doing flowers and then he reprimands a young man for doing the border of his print first.
2:25	He is watching everyone else and still hasn't begun his project.		The teacher tries to be amusing but in my eyes is *very* sarcastic. He
2:30	He finally begins and makes 12 finger prints which he tells his friend represents a dozen eggs. He works very slowly.		remarked that this was a good project for these students because they would know what to do when the police took them to be fingerprinted.
2:45	He is talking with a friend and says "this is boring"		

End-of-Day Interview

1. *Assume that a new kid moved next door and would be your schoolmate. What are three good things about this school that you would tell him/her?*
   1. There is not much homework.
   2. The contests and activities at school are fun.
   3. The library has a lot of good books.

2. *What are three things about this school that you would change, if you could?*
   1. The dress code—it is too strict.
   2. Pay the teachers more so they would be *happier!*
   3. Teach all students "truth."

3. *How do you feel, in general, about your teachers?*
   "They are okay—I guess they try their best."

4. *Is there a person in this school that you would readily turn to for help on a personal problem?*
   Yes, Mr. _____, my Social Studies teacher. (He is also his A/A teacher.)

5. *How do you feel about the way students treat one another?*
   "They try to play a role—try to impress one another and some think they are better than others. Most students are selfish."

6. *How do you feel, in general, about your classes? Do they challenge you?*
   "They are hard for some people but they are *real* easy for me."

7. *Do you have opportunities to help make decisions abou what goes on in class?*
   "Not really. In A/A we are asked what we would like to change but even if the majority wanted something changed the principal wouldn't listen."

I asked him the following additional questions:

—*Do you enjoy A/A?*

"I used to but now it is just a study hall. We don't do any neat activities."

—*What class did you enjoy most today?*

"P.E."

—*What class did you not enjoy?*

"Art."

—*Why?*

"The art teacher doesn't explain things real well—I always have to ask my buddy because he's good in art. The art teacher always seems mad."

Shadow Study Number 5
A 6-8 middle school with interdisciplinary teaming

Time	Specific behavior at 5-7 minute intervals	Environment	Impression-Comments
8:20		Bell for school entry. Students who had assembled outside or in hall just inside school doors surged into the halls to lockers. Home room students settled in.	The principal at this point, walked me (counter-traffic) down the hall to my student's home room. He left me with the homeroom teacher, who quietly pointed out G. Students were generally business-like, not too noisy or boisterous. Occupied with arranging books. Not particularly noticing me as visitor.
8:30	G. settled, arranged her books at her desk.	Tardy bell. Teacher emphasized quiet. Students were quiet. Announcements by principal over P.A. system. Very faint, hard to hear.	There were 23 students in home room. My first impression of the student I was to "shadow" was that she was a very nice *little* girl. She had on blue jeans; a light blue, long-sleeved sweatshirt.
8:33	She passed the home room time sitting on her knees at her desk, playing with her purse, talking a bit with a girl behind her.	Teacher asked if everyone were set for "International Day" tomorrow— no comments returned.	She kept her reading glasses inside purse, taking them out for close work of reading and writing, but not constant wear. Sort of random. Her hair was about shoulder length, attractively cut, loose, not in face.

Time	Specific behavior at 5-7 minute intervals	Environment	Impression-Comments
		Students were quiet, but some quietly talked after announcements which seemingly was allowed, though cautiously.	
8:35		Teacher: "Line up at the door." Bell: "All right." And students filed out to go to first class.	I gathered the reins were tightly held by the teacher.
8:40	G. went directly to class and to her seat.	First Period Science Class.	When I asked teacher where I should sit she said it was a "full class," so I found a place comfortably at the rear. She seemed as unsure and vulnerable under a stern unsmiling face, to students, as she was to me. 27 students —12 boys,15 girls —(I *think*! Some are hard to tell) These were table desks, two portable. The seating was obviously arranged by teacher for minimum interaction.
8:42	Sitting on one leg. Dropped paper. Went for it. Raised hand as teacher asked questions. G. was called on once and answered correctly.	Teacher began by seriously asking perfunctory questions about vernal equinox. Homework papers exchanged according to directions. Teacher read the question. Called on students by name to answer. Grade by "Put correct number over 13." "Pass forward, please." Teacher: "I told you we'd have lots and lots of writing."— Groans—"Oh, no. . ." Teacher closes door, hands out papers.	Remonstrance is not loud or prolonged. Just human!
	G. gets pencil out of purse	"You need 2 sheets of this. . . more before we are over . . ."	Whole class is very obedient.

Time	Specific behavior at 5-7 minute intervals	Environment	Impression-Comments
		"Bring left-overs back up." "I'd prefer that you use pencil. " "Supposed to do that in home room."	
	Opens book.	"You need to have book open to Pre Cambrian."	
8:50	Begins to copy answer as teacher talks. Others seem to wait. Erases. Yawns. Taps pencil. Swings legs.	Teacher asks some questions from paper. "What does 'pre' mean?" "Write down your answer."	
9:00	Works away. Purse is on desk at elbow, sort of like a comfort/shield.	Class continues copying answers from books onto columned sheets. Teacher walks back and forth, mostly at front of room and part way down two aisles.	All seem absorbed in writing. What a good friend a purse is! Sort of like a stuffed animal.
9:01	G. raises hand for most questions.	Teacher begins to ask for answers from their papers. "If you don't have it, write it down."	Students come out with correct answers.
9:05	She seems to be thinking with the teacher. Raises hand.	Teacher: "I'm thinking of a word. You wouldn't be driving a car today without this." Student: "Oil?" "Not what I was thinking. Iron ore. Teacher shows pull-down map Minnesota to Cleveland, route of iron ore. "Is pre-Cambrian." "What else is made of steel?" They name a few items like lockers, pots and pans . . . A boy asks if neck-	Many raise hands; want to participate. (Why does this fool us that learning is taking place?) They are *not* driving yet! She's trying to relate, but is hesitant and not clear, so I wonder if students made any connection at all. They just answered to stay alive and awake! Unrelated, but teacher does acknowledge question and turns it to class. It isn't really answered. Her personal comment seemed to
9:10	G. does not talk, in the buzz, with her boy seat-mate.	laces are made of gold. Then teacher says she is allergic to nickel in earrings. "All right, boys and girls. . ."	escape her protective armor, and soon she attempted to regain control of the resulting buzz of talk in the room.

Time	Specific behavior at 5-7 minute intervals	Environment	Impression-Comments
9:12	She does not write; probably already had answered all questions. She sits and swings her feet.	"Put your papers in your folder."	Class is allowed to chat last minute before bell rings.
9:19	G. was near the door and I lost her, but I knew she was ahead, hurrying down the crowded hall. She was already seated in her next class when I arrived.	Bell rings and class is allowed to go. Second period. Social Studies.	Ah! A different arrangement of desks! 27 students—10 boys, 17 girls. Each half faced the other half, three desks deep on each side. The teacher worked mostly from near her desk, but also walked down the middle aisle.
9:22	G. raises hand right away. "I don't have any relatives coming."	Teacher begins by giving instructions for International Day to be held tomorrow. Refers to a paper sent home previously to parents. Teacher re-assures that many parents cannot come; they work.	She had laryngitis and talked softly—until she was angry. She came across as forced gentleness covering great tension, apt to snap. As Chairman of next day's events, she probably felt pressure.
9:28	G. asks again about where to go if no parents; are those students allowed to go.	Other hands go up; "Do you have to eat own food?" "Where do we put food in morning?" Teacher then takes class to cafeteria where International Day is to be held.	It seems to bother G. about no guests and where that left her. I wonder why no student planning was done. It's all or-ganized by the teacher, who tells them.
9:30	G. runs ahead to be at head of line. In the cafeteria she stands alone, by the wall, close to table where teacher is ex-plaining. She listens attentively.	Teacher gives directions for tomor-row about placement of maps and food.	Several boys "goof off" and hit and are called back by teacher but are generally well-behaved.
9:32	G. helps, with 3 others, put the table back. She goes out first, with teacher.	Back down hall to return to class. In classroom again, teacher hands out folders and calls students one by one to front to receive graded salt map.	Students are reasonably quiet. Teacher is obviously anxious about time.
9:45	G. is at teacher's desk longer than other students, and then comes back to her desk,		

72

Time	Specific behavior at 5-7 minute intervals	Environment	Impression-Comments
	troubled, carrying her salt map. To no one in particular, but maybe neighbor she says: "Look what she's done—she took out my mountains."		
	She muses. Sits quietly. Purse hanging on chair.	Folders are directed to be placed on back table.	Teacher is anxiously stacking folders. I notice that G. is upset and unhappy
9:50	G. raises hand again: "Does my map count against me?"	Teachers does answer to assure her. It was graded last week before this. It was an unfortunate accident. We'll make some dough and fill in.	about whatever happened to her map. She is not afraid to ask again.
9:52	G. gets right to work, as all do. After a while she gets out glasses to wear. She works easily. Seems content.	Work sheets are handed out. End of Class.	More of those fill-in-the-blanks busy work!
10:02	G. dashes to her locker, then comes back past me to go to gym. I ask several girls to show me, including G.	Third period. Phys Ed, called "Gym." A long walk down the hall to the girls' locker room; then out to half the gym.	While most students took me as a visitor, for granted, ones nearby were curious and friendly. I tried to convey assurance to them, taking an interest in them, always keeping alert to how things
10:05	G. changed her jeans and sweat shirt to the standard yellow top and black shorts. All girls were in open area changing quickly.		looked through my special friend's experiences. This time, in the locker room, I did not want to embarrass the girls by my presence, but I was concerned by the lack of privacy afforded girls as they changed clothes, for gym in an open, public space.
10:10	G. had been in a group in the gym near a bulletin board. She lingered longest, reading the posted items.	Girls and boys, under a woman teacher, spread over the area for exercises. A boy student first called directions.	The usual, "one, two, three, four," counted. I noticed one girl did not do sit-ups, so guess individual needs are considered.
10:17	G., with others, comes for her badminton racquet. "Get the good one," she says, to no one	Teacher announces badminton team scores and gives direc-	They take turns playing, as only 4—or 2 per team—can play at once.

73

Time	Specific behavior at 5-7 minute intervals	Environment	Impression-Comments
	in particular.	tions for the day. Teams form and play.	
	G. gets to play first. She enters in bouncily. Has trouble serving. Bird just falls.	About 8 on a team, each of 3 courts or 16 boys and girls times 3 = 48 kids.	
10:25	I ask her, "Is this fun?" She sparkles, "Yeah, but I'm so short, I miss the overhead ones." G. sits on bleachers, at side of her team's court. Shouts, raising hand, claps. "Out!" "We won! We won!" "Ya gotta *hit* it! Over the fence! Whee!" She moves down the bench. Watches intently.	Her turn is over for awhile.	I wonder if anyone has first practiced them on skills, how to hold racket, etc. It could have been age, but it looked hit and miss style.

G. concentrates on the activity. Is placid outside. If she wants/needs friends, she does |
10:35	Pushes away boy who is wigling around, keeping her eyes on the play. Her turn again to play. She smiles, occasionally.	Teams shift again.	not make overtures. I talk with girls about where they keep gym outfits.
10:40		Back to the locker room to change back to school clothes. End of class. Hall race to next class.	
10:45	G. walks with me. She says: Mr P. is funny. Depends on how he feels. He doesn't care if we are late. I ask: "Do you ever have to take showers?"—"No. My mother used to splash hair and hands wet to make them think she'd taken shower."		
10:48	She goes back down hall, after bell, to her locker, since Mr. P. was talking to me at doorway.	Fourth Period. Language Arts.	Teacher talks with me at doorway. I feel good about him, as he seems tuned in to kids. He came out (as if he trusted me— thanks!) with: "I like teaching; I don't like my job." He was giving me a message.
10:50	G. comes back in and class begins.	Students are more active and more talkative than in previous classes, more free, but respect teacher.	Students all get in; I find a seat. 24 students; 11 boys, 13 girls. The teacher moves around the front of the room, with walks down the aisles. He

74

Time	Specific behavior at 5-7 minute intervals	Environment	Impression-Comments
			is firm, clear in speaking, uses humor and emphasis. Brings students into his directions, explanations, questions. He listens to their comments and responds to them. It sounds like respectful rapport. He is personable and approachable.
10:55	G. has a front, middle seat. The teacher picks up her notebook for the current project and uses it as a class illustration.	Teacher says: "G. has a very neat, organized notebook. Ouch—it stabbed me! These spirals are not so good. She has properly labeled sections. She included the dittoes, as I asked. How nice! She also has a list in the front. That's called 'organization.'	I don't think he knew that G. is "my" student. He just knew how to compliment a student to make her feel good and to show a worthy example for others to see how *they* might do a notebook well.
	G. seems quietly pleased.	—Why not *use* it?"— and he hands it back. We are doing word study. Pro-mote . . . A student asks about "permote." Teacher uses opportunity to emphasize importance of proper pronunciation, not be sloppy in speaking which is why student had heard someone not pronouncing "promote" correctly.	Ah, teacher relates learning to where kids are!
11:00	G. quietly absorbs all this.	Teacher gives answers to homework as students look at papers. Teacher admits mistake in reading answer book. Student says, "can't be perfect!" Teacher says, "Even I." "Last week, I did. . . twice! So, we all make mistakes.	Teacher is human. Admits error. No wonder students say he understands them. I suspect teacher does not like to make students do so much paper work but is caught in the expectation
11:05		I'm sorry." "Speaking of English. . ." Stu-	trap of the system.

Time	Specific behavior at 5-7 minute intervals	Environment	Impression-Comments
		dents respond with "uugh's" "Come on. What mean by cumulative review?". . .	
11:10	G. asks a question (which I didn't hear, but she received an answer from teacher).	Teacher: "For homework. . ." Students, again, "Uugh. . ." Teacher: "I know, I assign too much." Student: "Oh no. You don't, really." Teacher: "I'm waiting for everyone's attention. Page 172. Exactly follow the directions. Students: "Uugh. . ." Teacher: "I assure you, you won't die of a heart attack. . .Page 173—do *not* write the sentence. . . There are 95. Two sheets of paper. S., I'll give you a sheet. 90% of success is following directions. The way you present is half the battle. That's why you are going to be neat, isn't it, L.?. . . Please do this test first. Then put it on back table. Then do homework. Don't worry about it; do one thing at a time Do *this* now.	Good strategy. He didn't buck them, and they responded in kind.
11:15			Teacher respects students' feelings but insists on correct procedure. Gives advice along the way. By the end of the year I am sure his students have something to remember. I thought about G., sitting on feet, perched on knees, swinging her feet. Suddenly I put myself in her body and realized—she is tiny, very short. Her feet cannot reach the floor! They dangle about 3 inches above it. How would I feel if *my* feet couldn't reach the floor from any of my school seats, all day long???
	G. tackles paper, sitting on feet.		
		Public address system loudly interrupts: "Can you tell me where ___ is?" Students all stop work. Some try to help answer.	What an annoyance to teacher and to students! I can see why the secretary did not know; there are errors in my student's schedule.
		Quiet established again. "There are people still working; be fair."	Boy in middle pokes girl ahead; she pokes back.

76

Time	Specific behavior at 5-7 minute intervals	Environment	Impression-Comments
11:25	G. goes up to ask teacher— probably about a recent test.	"Honey, not yet. I had ___ last night and don't have them done yet."	G. has asked other questions today. She appears calm outside, but I think she must be unsure inside and needful of reassurance.
11:28	G. is out the door quickly.	Bell ends the class.	
11:30	I lost her on rapid hall walk. She was in next room when I arrived.	Fifth period. Reading Class.	27 students: 11 boys, 16 girls.
11:35	Reads, sitting on both feet.	Teacher starts class with silent reading. During this, she circulates, distributing papers and talking with students.	I wonder if the teacher's presence over my shoulder and noisy heels on floor would assure or bother me, if I were G. It must be *hard* to not have feet able to touch floor!
11:40	Shifts book to lap, head on arm as she reads; feet dangle.		
11:45		Teacher gives students a choice: SRA now or later? Teacher read to them now or later? They vote to do SRA now and get it done. She reminds them no class for next two days— International Day.	A choice!
	G. asks a question: (raises hand) 2 days?	Teacher answers her: one day is 6th grade, but next day is 7th's.	
	G. puts on her reading glasses for the SRA test.	Teacher hands out reading cards.	
11:50	G. is in same position as for silent reading. Seems to finish in good time. Gets out paper to write answers.	They all do SRA.	All concentrate well. Teacher moves about, heels clacking.
12:00	Goes back to more SRA reading.	Bell at noon for other grade's lunch.	Students seem not distracted by hall noise. A few boys talk. Student body seems largely "middle class" children, clean, well dressed. Some girls mature. G. is a child by size. Some boys seem ready to burst into mischief; keep an eye on teacher;
12:10	Still at reading card. Writing answers.		

Time	Specific behavior at 5-7 minute intervals	Environment	Impression-Comments
			restrain. A few act up when not watched.
12:12	Teacher bends over G.'s desk. G. talks, smiles briefly.	All work on SRA. Teacher announces "7 minutes left." "Put papers in folders."	This room is a social studies room by a teacher with this one reading class. There are salt maps, teacher made bulletin boards, some student papers, well displayed. Front board has homework supplies (an old list) supplies required "Weds., March 11. Red." (today's) Teacher circulates; smiles; then sits at front of room to read story to class, aloud. I wonder how many are really listening to the story. They seem to be. It is about a supposed end of the earth, so they are engrossed.
12:14	G. gathers her things. Takes off glasses; sits on knees. G. raises hand, with about 10 others. Answers one question when called on.	Teacher directs class. Teacher asks questions related to story, about 4 years before earth's atmosphere is destroyed. Teacher reads. Students listen well.	
12:20	G. builds a book tent as teacher reads, but listens.		
12:27		End of class. Teacher oversees students to hall as they go out to lunch.	
12:30	G. went to her locker, got her sack lunch, came back past me on her way into the cafeteria. She sat in the middle with 3 other girls.	Lunch, in the Cafeteria. A large room.	I talked with the Guidance Counselor who has this duty daily, along with 2 "room mothers" who watch. When students raise hand, the adults recognize and nod, meaning they may get up—to go for more food or to go out to the gym.
12:45	Though most students left, G. and her friends slowly ate and made no move to leave. They didn't talk a lot but were content to chat.		Deciding I might as well do it all, I went over and asked the 4 girls if I could sit with them. What could they say? I talked with them, mostly a girl beside G. who was seemingly happy to talk.
1:00	G. went down the hall, alone.	Bell, ending lunch period.	Most of room seemed well-behaved.
1:03	G. was ahead of me in the hall and in her class when I arrived.	Period Six: Arithmetic Class (This is the room with the teacher of her Home Room.)	I saw G. into class, then I made my restroom stop—way back down hall to the girls' rest room. Big, barn-y. Some writing on walls.

78

Time	Specific behavior at 5-7 minute intervals	Environment	Impression-Comments
			Doors, but no latch.
			How can students ever use the rest room? It is so far away, not on their hall route. Besides, there is no time, and there is pressure to not be late.
1:10	G. and class started paper work. All class quiet and working.	Teacher gave directions in a loud voice. Students worked on papers, which was like a test to be given tomorrow.	21 students; 10 boys, 11 girls. Homework and class rules on a poster. Also note "Learn to Love Math. It's Part of Your Future." This is motivation for 6th graders?!
1:23	Still working. Feet swinging.		
1:25	G. stood up. Opened purse. Checked another's traded paper. Glasses on.	"Stop. Collect from back. (exchange) Put first and last name on paper." Teacher used overhead projector, reading answers.	
	G. walked over close to screen to look at overhead projection.	Image was *dim.* "Pens under the desk. Total wrong at the top."	
	Yawning. Looked tired. Answered with class as worked out on board by teacher. Raised hand —"too many sets."	"If you had a perfect paper put it on my desk: We'll go over. How many missed #1? 3 1/2 bananas. . . G. called on by teacher, from among about 8 raised hands.	
1:35	Yawning covered. Sitting sideways to see board, on one leg.	"Tomorrow, quiz."	
1:40	Heads for chalkboard before her row is called when she sees intention. She works problems. Boy next to her talks to her. She talks about problem with him. He seems to help. She smiles. Stays on task. Erases carefully, smoothing it out. Then works next problem.	Board work by everyone in class. Teacher circulates, checking each student. Points out a correction to G.	
1:43	Hastily picks up things as bell rings.	Bell. End of class.	
1:47	G. and another girl walked with me, and I had to ask directly which class G. was going to. She was probably wondering, but nice.	Seventh Period. Art Class. It was a long hike in a hurry. Boys nearly crashed us in the hall.	My schedule said "Health" was next, but, in walking down hall, I discovered G. was going to Art, so I'm glad I walked with her this time.

79

Time	Specific behavior at 5-7 minute intervals	Environment	Impression-Comments
		Students went to seats, but were noisier than in other classes.	A typical art room. Large tables, chairs. Paper and clay work around. 16 students: 7 boys, 9 girls.
1:50	G. watches teacher. Smiles admiringly, curiously, at her.	Teacher began by talking about "Shade of color is a hue," as a way to lead into handing out papers to be done "as extra credit" while she took one student at a time to wash blank ink off a drawing, painting, each had done, `a la a French method. "Do your work quietly as I	
2:00		do mine." Teacher does "washing" of papers, one at a time.	I circulated and watched. A girl volunteered to tell me about ceramic "Big Mouths." G's was very creative, I thought, maybe "the best." Some kids "goof off."
2:07	G. shows me her "Big Mouth" ceramic work. I admire it. "It is a monster. Monsters eat people, so here is a girl being eaten. Her leg is lying there, severed."		
	Talks with girl at same table, as she writes answers on sheet.		Busy work, methinks! They know it.
	G. goes to look at ceramic work. Studies it carefully. Looks in dictionary (to find answer?)		
2:15	G. has her turn to wash off her painting. It turns out well. She said, "I had hair on her." (not evident now.)		Hers actually is very good. She seems to be artistic. I think she is a perfectionist. This is the second time today she is troubled by an imperfection she thinks not her fault.
2:25	We admire results as they dry in hall. G. volunteers an answer.	Teacher goes hurriedly over answers. Students don't much care.	
2:27		Bell. End of class.	
2:28	G. walks with me, knowing I'm going back to her home-room for "Directed Study." She says to me (as if I were a student) "Don't be late; you'll get an essay to write from Ms. J." So, we hurry!	Eighth Period. Directed Study. In the same room as home room and also Arithmetic. But something different is happening today.	This surprises me and I ask some girls what is going on. "We're going to the cafeteria to practice the music for tomorrow's International Day." So I chat a bit. "When do you

80

Time	Specific behavior at 5-7 minute intervals	Environment	Impression-Comments
		"Girls line up! Boys line up!" We rush down the hall then stand in line outside the cafeteria.	girls ever go to the rest-room? You're always rushing!" "Oh, you don't. You get used to it. You don't drink water. You *can* ask for a pass. You get used to it."
2:30	G. pulls way back alone. I ask her about it. "Oh, I'm the shortest, so I'm last, so I just wait." G. goes last and takes her place at left front row.	Someone orders them in, and they march, single file, onto the risers. Suddenly, a teacher flares up at a boy, pointing angrily at him, bawling him out badly—for what? Other teachers roll their eyes. Kids look and act scared.	I was concerned about how and when I could reveal to G. what I had been doing and interview her. I asked a teacher. "Get her now." So we did.
2:35	Teacher goes to call her out.		I walked out with her, assuring her of a "happy surprise" so she would would not fear.
2:37	She walks out with me. Her fact is a wreath of smiles.		
3:15	She walked, danced on air! All smiles.	Interview, til after school ends as walks.	We found a quiet office to talk.

End-of-Day Interview

1. *Assume that a new kid moved next door and would be your schoolmate. What are three good things about this school that you would tell him/her?*

They have it well-organized.
At the beginning of the year, they understood at first if you were late.
Kids are not snobby. (?—later, contradicts)

2. *What are three things about this school that you would change, if you could?*

Keep people from making fun of you.
Make time for rest room. Put in more rest rooms.
Let kids pick own teachers.
Have longer lunch period. But hate to go to gym, sit on bleachers.
Would like to be a one-room school with one nice teacher (as where she came from!)
Would change some of kids, who make fun of teacher.
I was hit on head with locker, had to go to nurse.
Hall pushing.
Have math second period. (?)

3. *How do you feel, in general, about your teachers?*

Some I really like.
Some don't pay any attention; raise hand; they don't see me.
They just say it and expect you to know it. (!)

81

4. *Is there a person in this school that you would readily turn to for help on a personal problem?*

Maybe the girl you saw me eating lunch with, _____. (One of group of 3 at lunch table)

5. *How do you feel about the way students treat one another?*

They have own group of friends. Shut people out. Some shove people around.

6. *How do you feel, in general, about your classes? Do they challenge you?*

Some help me learn. Others don't explain.

7. *Do you have opportunities to help make decisions about what goes on in class?*

—No.

I noticed one teacher asked you to choose which one first.

—Oh, they are *little* choices. Ones that *are* given just lead to a dead end.

NOTE: The analyst's reactions to this shadow study are especially perceptive, poignant, and powerful. They are incorporated in Chapter 6 as a part of the summary and conclusions.

Shadow Study Number 6

A 6-8 middle school with full departmentalization

Time	Specific behavior at 5-7 minute intervals	Environment	Impression-Comments
8:15	Reading "Say No To Drugs" pamphlet. Picking at fingernails. Talking to girl next to her. Smoothing hair. Watching teacher interacting with others. Talking to neighbor. Reading pamphlet. Sitting quietly as others buy things from "store."	Homeroom class— loud teacher, barking orders, but in friendly manner.	This is just a place to kill time until first period starts.
8:22	Sitting quietly, picking at fingernails, biting nails. Put pamphlet away in pencil case of notebook. Got up to go to pencil sharpener. Put sharpened pencil back in pencil case. Sitting quietly.		Notebook neatly organized.
8:29	Talking to neighbor quietly. Looking at poster of male star on front of friend's notebook. Showing picture on front of her notebook. Sitting quietly watching other students. Got up to return teacher's tape after using a piece to tape corner of torn book cover. Reading quietly. Talking excitedly to neighbor. Looking through a sheaf of folded paper while talking to neighbor.		Other students noisy.

Time	Specific behavior at 5-7 minute intervals	Environment	Impression-Comments
8:36	Still talking quietly to neighbor. Rearranging pictures in front of notebook cover. Picking up books on floor and stacking things up in preparation for the bell. Put quietly purse on shoulder. Sat talking to neighbor waiting for bell.		Others wandering around, talking in groups.
8:40	Walks along to next class in gym. Enters locker room and dresses alone, does not interact with anyone.	Dismissal bell rings Locker room.	
8:46	Enter gym. Gets drink. Sits in bleachers between two girls. Talks quietly. Listens to those talking. After roll check, gets up and walks across gym to sit in formation on gym floor. Pushing hair back and straightening it. Sits quietly, paying attention. Follows teacher directions. Does warm up exercises as directed and counts out loud as directed.	Gym class. First period.	
8:53	Sits quietly while boys run laps. Girls get up and run laps. Student runs alone. Does not talk to others. Continues to run when others are walking. Girls exit to the other gym. Sits in line along wall. Student sits among others, talking quietly to neighbor. Others walk on to volleyball court. Student stays seated waiting her turn. Picking at her knee. Picking at fingernails. Sits with arms hugging knees, chin on knees. Looks up at game. No reaction to game apparent.		Others sitting in small groups, talking. Others talking and laughing out loud.
9:01	Plays with watch, yawns. Teams change, but student still waiting for her turn. Still sits quietly. No apparent reaction to game. Explains something to neighbor, smiles. Uses gestures. Stretches legs out, then crosses them. Talks to neighbor, pointing and gesturing, possibly about game. Listening to neighbor talk.		
9:08	Talking quietly, yawning. Teams change. Student goes on court,		

Time	Specific behavior at 5-7 minute intervals	Environment	Impression-Comments
	in center. Looks around, watches placement of others on court. Pulls shirt down. Attentive to game, eyes on ball. Yawns. Makes catch in game and returns ball. No reaction. Makes another catch and return. Others respond positively. No reaction from student. Yawns. Watches ball. Smiles when other team misses. Claps and stands on tiptoe when other team misses. Stands with clasped hands waiting for ball. Smiles at teammate who makes a catch. Claps when other team misses. Smiles and runs forward as ball comes toward her. Serves ball, smiles. Smiles when other team fails to return ball.		Others doing cheerleader jumps, yelling, and clapping.
9:15	Talks to neighbor—something about her arm. Holding wrist as if it hurts, but still attentive to game. Game point announced. Student says something to all teammates. Disappointed when point is lost. Goes to wall and watches next game. Checks nails. Gets up when told by teacher and joins others on other wall of gym.		Others laughing out loud, talking, clapping, chants.
9:23	Doing fingering motions in the air like for piano. Walks quietly back to locker room. Dresses without talking to anyone. Wearing purple shorts under her jeans. Walks alone to next class. Smooths hair as walking.	Gym Locker room. Sidewalk between buildings.	
9:31	Arrives in class. Sits down. Gets assignment out of notebook, pencil from pencil bag. Speaks to neighbor. Sits quietly as teacher gives directions. Checks papers as students give answers. Takes off jacket.	On level math class— second period.	Sits in middle of classroom.
9:38	Checks paper and makes corrections as directed by teacher. Talks quietly when neighbor asks her a question. Checks fingernails, pats barrettes in hair. Points out something on other neighbor's paper. Messing with hair.		

84

Time	Specific behavior at 5-7 minute intervals	Environment	Impression-Comments
9:45	Listening as teacher gives answers and calls on students to give answers. Smooths hair. Gets out a red pen and loans to neighbor.		
9:52	Still listening, clicking pen. Called on to give answer. Gave correct answer. Continues to check paper. Plays with finger-nails. Attentive to overhead and chalkboard when teacher writes.	Math Class	No positive response from teacher, just went on to next student.
10:00	Still sitting quietly while check-ing answers. Drumming fingers on desk. Raises hand. Asks for answer to be repeated, but it was one that was beyond the required assignment. Counted up score. Turned in paper. Put red pen back in bag and her checking pen. Opens text. Gets out extra pencil for neighbor. Opens notebook to get paper. Puts head on hand, stares at paper.	Teacher is explaining new problem.	Seemed to get most answers correct.
10:07	Head on desk, not paying atten-tion. Raises head, checks bar-rette in hair, puts head back on desk. Raises head and holds hands over eyes for a second. Yawns. Head back on desk. Looks up when neighbor is called on. Chin on books, eyes closed for a second. Head up, yawns. Watches teacher and mouths answer to problem, but does not volunteer. Staring straight ahead, yawns. Head on desk. Head up. Shakes head about "Are there any more ques-tions?" Head on hands looking down. Looks up to watch teacher. Head on desk. Head up. Scoots back, head on desk. Head up. Smiles. Heads paper. Yawns. Writes down assignment. Starts on homework assignment.	Teacher works problems on board. Teacher says only 5 minutes left, so head paper for homework. Gives assignment.	
10:14	Works on first few problems. Called on for answer. Gave answer.	Teacher checks first 3 answers with kids.	Teacher comes to talk to me, tells me S. will be recommended for above level math for next year.

Time	Specific behavior at 5-7 minute intervals	Environment	Impression-Comments
10:20	Packs up things. Puts away pencil, etc. Puts on jacket. Gathers up things and leaves, alone. Walks to next alone.	Bell rings.	Seems to be very organized.
10:25	Sits down at table. Straightens hair. Makes face at reading speed mentioned. Looks at screen at story and reads silently. Finishes reading. Gets up for Kleenex. Blots at ear. Student mimics another student who is waving hand in the air. Smiles and neighbor she is imitating smiles back.	Reading class—third period. Teacher gives instructions for controlled reader activity. Other students doing answers to story questions.	Speed seems to be a challenge to S.
10:31	Works on questions. Finishes. Checks over answers. Heads paper. Copies assignment. Writes vocabulary words. Blots ear while reading.	Teacher calls out answers. Teacher gives today's assignment, tells students to head paper.	Head very close to paper as writing—vision?
10:38	Works on definitions independently. Talks and laughs quietly point with neighbor, then right back on task.		
10:45	Still on task. Finishes work, blots ear again. Works on a puzzle or something until others finish. Reads controlled reader story on screen. Finishes story. Begins work on questions.	Teacher turns on controlled reader again.	
10:52	Still on task. Then reread story from screen at faster speed. Reads with hands on either side of face, elbows on table, looking intently at screen.		
11:00	Makes corrections on story questions. Opens book, rereading, looking at paper. Finished work, working on puzzle or word find waiting for others to finish. Checked answers to assignment. Looked back in book. Returned to work on puzzle. Looks up listens to teacher. Watches each student participates in oral.	Teacher giving directions for new activity.	Appeared to have missed very few.
11:07	Oral turn—gestures as participates listing words with a particular letter. Playing with hair. Watches other students participate,		Teacher tells me that student thinks I am following her.

Time	Specific behavior at 5-7 minute intervals	Environment	Impression-Comments
	smiles. Gathers things and gets up and leaves.	Bell rings.	
11:15	Getting out word list. Drumming fingers. Marks words on list as called out.	Language Arts Class-above level. Teacher dictates Teams word list for sentence writing and test on Friday.	Notebook seems to be neatly organized so she turns right to the word list needed—no hunting through a mess to find it. Sits at back of class.
11:20	Still on task. Puts away word list. Moves desk to be a partner with neighbor. Bites nails. Listens to teacher.	Teacher gives directions for activity. Students must move desks to be in pairs.	
11:25	Student listening and picking at nails. Got 100 on spelling test. Reads silently as another student reads out loud. Raises hand in response to question but not called on. More silent reading while another student reads out loud. Doing fingering exercises on desk top. Silent reading while oral is going on. Stays in class when given option of leaving early for lunch because of 100 on spelling test. Decides to go early the next day.	Teacher gives directions about essay contest. Reads names of 100s on spelling test.	
11:35	Still on task—reading.		
11:40	Left for lunch, alone.	Bell rings.	Student thinks I am following so I left ahead of and went on to cafeteria. I gather she went to her locker.
11:50	Entered cafeteria with lunchbox and one girl with her. Sat at a table with 3 or 4 others and ate lunch.		
12:00	Left cafeteria.		Again I do not follow because I do not want to raise suspicions
12:10	Standing alone outside classroom waiting for teacher to unlock. Moves to group of girls and visits.	Bell rings to return to Language Arts Class.	
12:15	Listens to teacher. Closes eyes and "dances" back and forth to to invisible beat. Takes off jacket. Picks at fingernails.	Teacher reads sample essays from 7th grade.	
12:22	Looking around, playing with fingers.		

Time	Specific behavior at 5-7 minute intervals	Environment	Impression-Comments
12:27	Gets out pencil and paper and begins to write. Neighbor talks to her, she answers quietly. Continues writing.	Teacher assigns essay and gives remainder of class to work.	Others talking quietly, brushing hair.
12:34	Still on task. Neighbor interrupts, but then right back on task.		
12:40	Leaves room with books and lunchbox and student who was in her class.	Teacher reviews assignment and tells students to put away. Bell rings.	
12:45	Gets notes out on desk to review for test the next day. Playing with barrette in hair. Raises hand, but not called on. Raises hand again, was recognized again, read information requested. Neighbor asked for her notes, she passed them over. Got them right back. Copied notes from overhead.	Bell rings for social studies class.	Sits at back of class.
12:50	Broke pencil lead and made a noise that caused two others to look around. Took off jacket. Wiggling in desk, wiping hands on and off jeans, swinging arms. Copied additional notes.	Teacher put more notes on overhead.	
12:55	Still on task. Student opens book. Writes info teacher suggests. Then reads along in book as teacher talks about important points in chapter for test.	Teacher opens book to p. 162 to review.	I'm about to fall asleep.
1:00	Turns pages in book as teacher points out important info.	Teacher giving review info and calling on students to produce info.	
1:05	Called on to give a definition. Answered correctly. Listening to review. Picking at nails. Called on to give another answer. Did so correctly.	Going over Finding Fact questions aloud.	
1:10	Volunteered to answer, but not called on. Volunteered again, recognized and answered correctly. Volunteered but not recognized. Volunteered again, answered correctly.		

Time	Specific behavior at 5-7 minute intervals	Environment	Impression-Comments
1:15	Volunteered again, but not re-cognized. Volunteered again, responded correctly. Listens to each student as they say vocabulary words. Gave defini-tion when it was her turn.	Teacher praises good answer. Assigned vocabulary word to each student to say and define in turn.	Only time student got positive rein-forcement from a teacher all day.
1:21	Talks quietly with one neighbor. Going over review questions for test.	Teacher assigned some-one to put crossword on board while others study quietly.	
1:25	Volunteered to answer cross-word question. Volunteered again. Volunteered, was recog-nized, was incorrect. Put jacket on.	Student demonstrated crossword on board.	This has been the only class all day where only student has been actively seeking to be involved.
1:30	Left for next class with girl who had sat next to her.	Bell rings.	
1:35	Sitting in desk waiting for in-structions. Gets out materials for assignment.	Bell rings for science Some students leave to go to lab to get models as others get out ma-terials.	Sits at back of class.
1:37	Listens to teacher speak. Looks at other students. Volunteers to answer questions. Volunteers again. Plays with hair.		
1:44	Bites nails. Leans head on hand, closes eyes momentarily. Leaves class to go to lab.		
1:49	Return to class with model. Sits at desk. Tries to put a part of the model back together. Puts model on floor and turns in text to where other students are. Volunteers to answer questions. Volunteers again, waving hand. Hand back down, playing with hair and barrette.	Teacher still discussing lesson—students volun-teering answers to her questions.	
1:54	Takes jacket off. Plays with hands, making signs out in front of her face. Looks out window.		
2:00	Called on to answer question. Gives answer and expands it when teacher requests. Plays with hair. Sits quietly waiting for discussion to begin again. Plays with watch. Looks out window.	More students enter from lab. Then back to discussion.	

89

Time	Specific behavior at 5-7 minute intervals	Environment	Impression-Comments
2:05	Eyes closed momentarily. Turns page to next page of discussion. Shakes head, looks through cupped hands, like binoculars.		
2:10	Turns to next page. Rearranges pictures in front of notebook cover. Plays with glitter dots on desk from model. Continues to move hands and scratch head.	Teacher walks toward her desk to see what is going on.	
2:20	Stacks model on books. Leaves.	Bell rings.	I'm glad this class is over, and I think she is too.
2:23	Arrives in band hall, gets instrument (flute).		
2:25	Listens to teacher make announcements. Warms up.	Bell rings for band class.	
2:30	Playing scales as directed.		
2:35	Playing song as directed.		
2:40	Playing as directed.		
2:45	Sits quietly and fingers along without producing sound while another section plays.		
2:50	Playing as directed.		
2:55	Playing as directed.		
3:00	Playing as directed. Leaves class with observer to complete interview.		

End-of-Day Interview

1. *Assume that a new kid moved next door and would be your schoolmate. What are three good things about this school that you would tell him/her?*

   Teachers are nice. Some of the kids are nice—most of the sixth graders are.

2. *What are three things about this school that you would change, if you could?*

   Dress code—I hate it, long-tailed shirts made to wear out. Longer lunch—some people have to wait a long time in line. Ten minutes between classes—if you stay after class, it's enough time to get to next class.

3. *How do you feel, in general, about your teachers?*

   They're nice, except Mrs. M. is a little strict. Mrs. W. is my favorite.

4. *Is there a person in this school that you would readily turn to for help on a personal problem?*
   School nurse.

5. *How do you feel about the way students treat one another?*

   Most of the 7th graders bang people's heads against the wall, and hit each other with balls. I stay away from the Mexicans and the 7th grade boys. They are too rough.

6. *How do you feel, in general, about your classes? Do they challenge you?*

Don't like science. It is boring and she is picky. Math is too easy, a repeat of 5th grade. I like social studies because I like the projects.

7. *Do you have opportunities to help make decisions about what goes on in class?*

Only in Language Arts class. She gives us choices, lets us vote.

Shadow Study Number 7
A 6-12 middle school with departmentalization in sixth grade

Time	Specific behavior at 5-7 minute intervals	Environment	Impression-Comments
8:45	L. looked at flower model on display, chatted with friends.	Social studies/science first class of day— 2 blocked periods	Roll Call
8:50	Nodded head when teacher said, "Has everyone finished Chapter 1?"; cheered when spelling bee entrant left for competition; commented "That's sick" when teacher described interesting dead bug; questioned whether bug can switch to worm if worm can switch to bug. "Maybe a beetle crawled away, didn't like life in a box."	4 rows of desks; next-to-front seat. Assignment on blackboard.	Student chosen at random has already failed two years previously in school. Teacher collected news items about Africa, put them on bulletin board.
8:54	Left seat; looked at bugs on display at front of room. "Is the brown beetles the girl beetles?" Gave stick of gum playfully to neighbor. Got out book, searched for assignment; found paper; ripped it out; traded.		Teacher said get out Social Studies, trade papers to check in row.
8:57	L. answered question about African and black teeth; offered to look up information in *Geographic*; paged through dictionary.		Teacher discussing homework; boy not attending but still apparently getting answers.
9:04	L. left desk and moved to corner of room, selected *Geographic*, returned book to shelf behind teacher, returned to seat.		
9:06	L. answered teacher about hitting girl in head yesterday; said it was accident and he'd apologized.		Girl appeared droopy; when questioned, said L. had hit her yesterday.
9:10	Volunteered name of teacher who could check for concussion; described time teacher checked him. Reported oral grade of B on assignment. Showed teacher	Social Studies Class —1st period.	Teacher sent girl to office to be checked for concussion. Teacher had students call out grades on homework.

Time	Specific behavior at 5-7 minute intervals	Environment	Impression-Comments
	Geographic with African studies; got index to look up specific article.		
9:15	Defends self when teacher teasingly says he's reading everything else but ignoring African articles; continued to read *Geographic* while class looked at bugs.		Teacher stopped to feed bugs and discuss bugs. Asked about Henry the Navigator.
9:20	Got up and selected more *Geographics* after using index; teacher called him back to group and he returned to seat.		Discussed Vasco de Gama.
9:27	Raised hand and answered question about trade goods in Africa; discussed how silk frays so easily —wondered why leaders would wear silk; got excited making ship model for academic fair—added junks to discussion of sampans.		Digression on academic fair entries.
9:28	Raised hand, waved it and yelled "hoy"—tried to answer before teacher asked question . . . thought about Belgium ferry but wasn't the question.	Bell sounded for end of period . . . Announcements.	Sixth graders didn't change classes because of blocked periods.
9:31	Described boat he carved from locust bark . . . appeared interest- in teacher's discussion of boat model construction.	Social Studies class instruction.	
9:38	Held up hand to answer questions about British ferry; gave answers even though wasn't called on, answered teacher's question that Indonesia and India separate; offered to point out on map; got up to look at map; stood on chair to see map; helped to find by another student.		
9:42	Wisecracks, unacknowledged by teacher.		
9:45	Discussion of volcanoes; L. raised his hand to answer question about Mt. St. Helen's. . . interrupted teacher to ask question twice (ignored);	Social Studies class.	Class interrupted by messenger.
	raised hand; not acknowledged for four minutess; finally asked anyway about volcanic dusting causing rain.	Same classroom . . . switch to Science. Teacher turned out light.	Gave assignment. Teacher washed prism; switched to science; demonstrated light diffusion with

92

Time	Specific behavior at 5-7 minute intervals	Environment	Impression-Comments
			prism and an overhead projector.
9:51	Opened Science book.		
9:56	Poked student in front; apologized; teacher lost patience; said "L., no one can quite have the number of accidents with classmates you have." L. contributed gamma waves to discussion.		
10:05	Attending to discussion on light rays; picked up object from neighbor's desk . . . "pizza lamps" as an example of ultraviolet rays—"would that kill athlete's feet on your feet?"		
10:10	Volunteers information on what laser is . . . "Go for it, girls." L. raised hand to tell more about laser . . . smiled at teacher's criticism. . . said "I want to know if I'm right because I want to build one." "Can I tell you how I'd make mine, please, please? It won't take me 3 sentences." Hershey's kiss-shaped, crystal —shine through something.		Teacher asked girls to answer question. Teacher wouldn't let him answer. Class members said, "Shut up."
10:15	Watched teacher continuously during discussion.		
10:20	Asked time of neighbor. . . packed book bag. "Do you really have to have a license to own a laser beam?"		Teacher gave reading assignment.
10:21	Class ends. Stayed to talk to teacher. Asked where to get a prism. Went across hall to next class. L. went immediately to teacher's desk. Talked to girl. Examined pen pal list. L. chews gum, selects pen pal, talks to boy.	Science Classroom. Tables, microscopes along walls, etc. Seated near teacher with four other boys.	Directed study/activity period.
10:34	Filled out survey evaluating last activity—"Game Week" and evaluated past six weeks' choices.		Teacher moved around room while students filled out sheets.
10:40	Banged pen on table repeatedly to get it to write. Got up to throw pen away.		
10:45	Went to library. Checked out book.	Library	Teacher pinned picture on student's back . . . student had to get information from others and guess.

Time	Specific behavior at 5-7 minute intervals	Environment	Impression-Comments
10:55	Returned to directed study.		
11:05	Readying for dismissal from class . . . practicing walking on classmate's crutches.	Standing up in classroom with other students ready for dismissal from class.	
11:15	Reports to gym class for dressing out.	In locker room area.	Waited for L. to report to gym with classmates for actual start of class.
11:21	Reports to gym. Comes in running and goes immediately to his floor mat.	Gymnasium.	Readies himself immediately upon arrival.
11:28	Rolling across mat with classmates as part of practice of group routine.		
11:35	Working with classmates in group.	Gym . . . on mat with teacher's help.	Instruction to be provided by graduate student.
11:42	Part of pyramid/practice of routine on bottom.	Working with group on mat.	Seems active and cooperative.
11:49	Practicing on mat; talking.	With group on mat.	
11:56	Hopping on one foot while hanging on to partner while practicing routine.	Group on mat.	
12:02	Talking with instructor about routine.	With group on mat in gym.	Actively participating.
12:04	Sitting on mat with legs crossed as teacher brings closure to class.	All students sitting and quietly attending to teacher instruction.	Followed directions and worked well.
12:06	Line up and dismissal to locker room for dressing.		
12:11	Bell to lunch.	In hallway leading from gym to cafeteria.	Quietly waiting, taking his turn.
12:15	In line for lunch/bought school lunch.	Cafeteria.	
12:21	Paid for lunch/took seat amid friends talking.	Cafeteria line.	
12:28	Talking with friends.		
12:33	Carries tray up and goes outside in specified area to play with friends.	Seat at table with stationary seats on each side. Sits down between two boys.	

94

Time	Specific behavior at 5-7 minute intervals	Environment	Impression-Comments
12:45	Begins English class. Teacher stands to begin class—Announcements interrupt. . . calls 4 students from class. L. is one of 16 remaining.	L. is on Level 1 class (top level) in classroom with 5 rows approximately 6 seats each in end row, 2nd seat.	In class on time. Readies materials to start class.
12:47	L. asking girl in front of him for pen. Teacher calls him down for talking. He reports that "his pen gave way in 3rd period." The teacher asks who can share with him.	Seated in row. No student seated behind him or beside him.	Teacher stands at front of classroom and addresses group.
12:49	L. is reading book jacket of a library book while teacher reads announcement about writing contests.		
12:56	Teacher has assigned a couplet of poetry for students to mark rhythm showing division marks. L. says he is lost. He says the teacher lost him the last time she went over it. She says "try" since L. hasn't mentioned understanding before now.	English classroom with students seated completing desk work while teacher circulates.	L. shows little or no effort after he announces lack of understanding. He seems to merely copy the couplet from the board.
1:03	Teacher sends student to board to mark rhythm with stressed and unstressed syllables. She addresses L. directly to copy and follow the explanation carefully. He begins to speak and then silences himself.	Students at desk.	Seems to follow teacher's explanation and copies chart off board.
1:08	Teacher checks to see if homework has been done from workbook. L. is told to put library book away and gets out homework. Shows what he's done and reports "that's all I did."	Teacher circulates about room to check homework.	Teacher makes notations of some sort about degree of completion of assignment.
1:14	Going over sentences filling in predicate adjectives. L. offers that "The food looks *gross.*" The teacher discourages such a response and encourages L. to be positive.	Class exchange is interrupted with third intercom announcement.	Volunteered response but was not rewarded for correct response based on activity on hand.
1:20	L. called on to identify predicate adjective. Gets his response correct. Teacher moves on to next person.		Seems to tune in when it's his turn and he is told to find the predicate adjective in #10.

95

Time	Specific behavior at 5-7 minute intervals	Environment	Impression-Comments
1:25	Raises hand and asks question about nouns vs. pronouns based on example.		Teacher says his thinking is wrong but no explanation is offered to explain why.
1:30	L. looking at his pen while students go over worksheet answers as a large group. Even lowers head to desk though eyes are open. Gives little attention to what is going on.		
1:31	Class ends.		
1:35	Math class. When tardy bell sounds, some students are called from class by intercom. L. remains.	Class arranged with 6 rows, approximately 5 seats each. L. sits in the front seat of row 2, right under the teacher's eye, near teacher desk.	This is a 6.1 class (top level).
1:40	L. is called on to answer the first question. He is looking on the wrong page. The teacher asks him to look again, counting carefully; the students show him he is on the wrong page.		
1:45	When teacher moves on to new page of exercises to go over, L. pleasantly volunteers that he's already done these for them as this was the "wrong page" he was on earlier.		Though he doesn't always volunteer or appear to pay attention, L. knows what is going on around him.
1:52	Watching teacher as she demonstrates on board multiplying fractions.	Teacher using chalkboard as teaching tool.	Quiet as other students participate and volunteer answers.
1:57	With 24 minutes left in the period, teacher assigns classwork and homework . . . if students finish early they may work on their enrichment. L. asks an unrelated question about how long it takes a letter to get to Japan as he has a pen pal.	Teacher makes assignment and then begins to circulate about the room to assist individual students.	L. might ask an unrelated question but as soon as the teacher responds, he sets about completing the assignment individually.
2:03	Gets up and moves to teacher to ask if what he's tried so far is right.		
2:10	Continues working on assignment independently.	Flexibility of activities; students choose whether to work on classwork or enrichment.	Gets feedback and returns to seat as directed. Resumes work.

Time	Specific behavior at 5-7 minute intervals	Environment	Impression-Comments
2:12	Shuts book. Turns and begins to talk with neighbor. He is called down within seconds as wasting time; is instructed to get his enrichment folder and get started. He grins and asks the teacher if she can really look at this face and fuss. The teacher says she will refrain from answering. L. gets up and goes to find the enrichment folder.		
2:17	L. still trying to settle and find the right folder and materials. Says to teacher, "I know what you're thinking." She only returns a stare.		
2:21	Class ends.		
2:25	VOCAB class begins. . . . L. returns to the room and is in his seat when the tardy bell sounds.		
2:30	As teacher asks for volunteers to go over vocabulary, L. is looking at brochures on the Coast Guard.	L. remains in the same room as the last period, only one seat back from where he was. Students remain seated in rows while teacher stands at front of class.	L. mentioned to his Math teacher, between classes, that he was going into the Coast Guard when he gets out of school.
2:36	L. raises his hand and volunteers a response on vocabulary review. He is called upon and gets it correct.		Often seems to not be attending but then tunes in and directly addresses class activity.
2:41	Again, offers comical response. Teacher plays upon it and then continues.		Demonstrates sense of humor.
2:46	As teacher checks for homework, L. realizes that he has done the wrong assignment. Actually he has worked ahead of the rest of the class.		Teacher assures him that there is no problem, that he is just ahead.
2:51	As students sing song to review vocabulary, L. listens.		Seems selective about what activities he participates in.
2:55	L. leaves with observer to conduct interview.		

End-of-Day Interview

1. *Assume that a new kid moved next door and would be your schoolmate. What are three good things about this school that you would tell him/her?*

   1. It has pretty good food.
   2. Not so crowded.
   3. Has lots of clubs.
      (He got kicked out of 2 because of absences and not paying dues.)

2. *What are three things about this school that you would change, if you could?*

   1. A teacher.
   2. The food . . they should spend more money on it. . . hot dog sauce that looks the same as spaghetti sauce.
   3. More strict punishment. (Fighting; some penalty for first offenders)

3. *How do you feel, in general, about your teachers?*

   One makes me mad; one makes me glad; one makes me feel smart; and one makes me feel lazy. There is lots of variety and most are pretty good. One made him feel like he was not working as hard as he should.

4. *Is there a person in this school that you would readily turn to for help on a personal problem?*

   NO (here he was adamant in his response)

5. *How do you feel about the way students treat one another?*

   It's not really fair, most kids pick on a retarded student in school and that concerns him. Popularity and being accepted depends on who you are friends with . . . so there are a few people you need to be friends with if you want to be popular.

6. *How do you feel, in general, about your classes? Do they challenge you?*

   They are not challenging. Most are boring and teachers treat students in general like they are idiots. They speed through hard things and spend too much time on easy stuff.

7. *Do you have opportunities to help make decisions about what goes on in class?*

   NO! I would like input. It might work if students were in the right mood.

Selected Observers' Reactions

Self-Contained Situations

   The sixth grade is a remarkably well ordered, well taught, and humane place for students. I was impressed by the students' cooperation with their instructors and their generally courteous treatment of each other. Classes were very structured and content-oriented. I did not detect a great eagerness to learn, rather a willingness to be taught. My student had few opportunities to interact with his teacher or his classmates while in the learning environment. He answered several questions and twice asked for points of clarification; otherwise he was totally silent except for a little covert socializing. Although I do not have an elementary background I was surprised that the teachers did not do more with cooperative learning and encourage more in-depth discussion. The students appeared willing to do whatever was asked of them.

Quiet, Quiet, Quiet
Individual Seat Work—much of this

Rows and lines of students
Literal level thinking required for most of activities
Very limited instruction provided—rather assignment of "busy"/seat work tasks
Reading lesson was deplorable, instructionally speaking
No writing process instruction
Repetitive Day—*non* active or co-operative

Students generally were able to ignore me and accepted the response that I was an observer. My presence in class did not appear to disturb the normal activities or behavior of the shadowed student or his classmates.

This was an enjoyable day for me as I had a chance to shadow a sixth grader and gain some insight into his day. This sixth grader went through a pleasant day that included some interesting periods of time with very little boredom being displayed. The sixth grader I observed was a high middle student who followed all of the rules, on time, and with a smile. The group he was in was well behaved and typically cooperative. In this atmosphere he was unafraid to volunteer and join in. I do wish the recess time was better supervised so he would have had the opportunity to join in and build his confidence.

The atmosphere in the classes was very businesslike, safe, and caring. The students and teachers cared for and respected each other.

There appeared to be a somewhat restrictive atmosphere in this self-contained classroom. S. seemed mildly bored at times although she consistently raised her hand to answer questions, especially in subjects which she really seemed to like. This may have been due in part to the particular day of visitation, where there were no "special" subjects, except for Health, and where they did not leave the classroom except for recess and lunch. The teacher tried to get around this by moving her Math group out into the hall for instruction while an aide worked with the remainder of the children. The students did appear to be allowed to move freely about, so long as they didn't disturb anyone; and they did move at times to different groupings when subjects changed. There seemed to be a need for a release of energy between subjects in this very well-behaved class. S. is indeed privileged to enjoy the atmosphere of such a well-behaved classroom where respect seems to be a key factor. The students seemed to realize that they were primarily there to learn. There did not seem to be much social interaction within the class. The teacher seemed to have a good rapport with the class. The class size seemed a bit large and there was not much room for movement within the class. This restrictive factor and the self-contained factor seemed to be somewhat counteracted by the teacher's dedication to making learning fun by use of different projects, varied media, movement to other areas for book reports or small group instruction, use of plays, etc. The children seemed to understand the problem as well, and it was something they worked together to solve.

This student summed up her feelings about the school when she stated that she felt that everyone was doing everything they could to make school a positive experience for her. I would tend to agree with her.

A small six grade elementary school basically in hands of two teachers.

The sixth graders in this school "live" in a warm, caring, and nurturing environment. Their two teachers treat them with respect and interrelate with them positively and rationally—in fact, the teachers are very "low keyed" *but* very much in control of

99

their classes. Students appear comfortable —free to express and free to take risks academically—even if they are incorrect in response. Attempts at bizarre or blatantly disruptive behaviors (*minimal*) are deliberately acknowledged and dealt with in matter-of-fact fashion by the teachers. The academic day is rapidly paced, integrated, and varied. Positive reinforcements and rewards are emphasized. Spontaneity and flexibility seem to be the key to both teachers' camaraderie with the students. Role modeling by teachers is excellent, and the principal, who was a counselor is, indeed, a counselor here as well as a principal. Both teachers work beautifully as a team, and they are close to their principal.

The missing ingredients are: (1) Exploratory—especially "hands on"—activities. Students spend most of their day at their desks—and (2) lack of counseling support staff. There are obvious needs for a counselor—both for individuals and groups, especially because the students are at such a workable age and have such a good trust relationship with their teachers.

My greatest concern is the brutally abrupt transition these children—transescents, if you will—must make into a *"junior* high" school enviroment where there are 700-1,000 students, seven class periods and six periods with different non-teamed teachers, lockers, 12 to 15-year-olds expected to harmoniously associate, and virtually *no* readiness for any of this. That is why local schools are attempting to "integrate" middle school concepts, especially homeroom activity period, and are focusing tremendous efforts and dollars on this reorganization. I am vitally concerned about the well-being of these super sixth graders, and I am totally exhausted from my day in tranquillity—something the sixth grade teachers couldn't believe I deem tranquil.

Teamed Situations

I witnessed a young female student have the opportunity to experience many facets of an excellent educational process primarily sponsored by four teachers during my one-day stint. Maybe my perceptions were somewhat distorted from the fact that I was shadowing a younger age student than I typically work with, or the fact that the school size is much smaller than I'm used to, but regardless of possible biases, I saw very caring and firm teachers, good variety of curriculum, strong opportunity for increasing one's self-esteem, sufficient socialization inside and outside class time, excellent outlet for creative responses, and a positive environment to learn without fear of ostracism from any particular peer group.

A student in grade six seems to be exposed to many instructional experiences, a variety of adult personalities, and a generally pleasant, rewarding school day. The seven class subject areas in this observation, provided a variety of instructional opportunities and experiences. Students seemed to have ample opportunity to interact with peers and also with the teacher. Rules and expectations were clearly presented and generally students seemed to follow them well.

For instruction, a sixth grade student seems to have a fairly standard program and some electives. The instruction seems organized and well planned. Although a variety of experiences seem available, a sixth grader seems to spend a majority of time in class listening or being expected to listen.

I have some serious concerns about the regimentation of a six or seven-period day for this age group. As an adult, it was difficult to stay seated, rush between classes, to only be able to use the bathroom when someone else decided we needed to, sit at an assigned table at lunch with no chance throughout the day to run or just work off some energy. One can only guess at the frustration of an 11 or 12-year old. A day like this is a good reason to look at flexible scheduling and built in physical activity for every day.

As I approached the old school building which was nestled among low-income housing in a drab neighborhood, I wondered if my experience would confirm recent reports on the sorry state of our nation's schools. These feelings were short-lived, however.

Within the walls of the old building I found sixth graders and their teachers involved in learning, living, and obviously enjoying their schooling experiences. Not only were the rooms bright and cheerful, the total atmosphere surrounding the occupants was one of busy, happy noise uninterrupted throughout the day by bells or intercoms.

The idea of a cluster of 120 sixth graders divided into four groups and assigned to four teachers expresses the interest of the school's faculty and principal in moving toward a middle school organizational pattern. The interpersonal relationships observed between and among teachers and students, teachers and teachers, and students and students indicate an exceptional understanding of the needs of developing youngsters, especially sixth graders.

Although there were a few rough spots throughout the day of this sixth grader where learning experiences could be more effective for him, I came away with the feeling that this was a typical day, representative of a special year in his life.

The day spent observing a sixth grade student was quite rewarding. I happen to have a son in sixth grade, so the opportunity to learn more about what he experiences daily was a real opportunity. My son does not attend the same school in which I did the observation.

The school is viewed in the district as one that is quite steady, not too flashy or experimental but has a large number of excellent teachers who have taught in other schools prior to either transferring or being hired at this school.

From the student's perspective, the middle level concepts which were written in *Agenda for Excellence* are in many respects being implemented in the fifth and sixth grade teams. Students experience four teachers (on the average) in a given day for various subjects. Teachers have time to plan in the common fashion but are generally so busy preparing that they don't. There is not an expectation that joint planning occurs either.

I was feeling there was quite some difference between the boys and girls in the class. The girls appeared to be much more into looks, make-up, socializing, etc. than the boys. The boys appeared to me to be developmentally a year or two behind in that regard. They did not seem pretentious and did not pay much attention to the girls in their classroom, although there were one or two who obviously did. The students all wanted their individuality recognized both by peers and staff and the teachers in many cases met these needs.

I had a generally excellent feeling about the level of concern on the part of teachers for students. Students were treated with respect. The students' concerns were being met by the teachers.

I am thankful that the subject of my observations was very active; it may otherwise have been a bit dull. I found the sixth grade to be interesting and "educational." The students were involved, the teachers were involved, and the day passed quickly from one challenge to another. Though all the challenges were not academic, social challenges are also a part of growing up.

Teachers in the sixth grade are busy! Students are busy! During passing periods and breaks, the sixth grade area buzzes constantly . . . it's like watching a beehive. The business of sharing knowledge and information has to be just as active; fortunately it was!

Teachers and students knew what was expected of them. The day was what one might expect in a middle school. The atmosphere was one of warmth and caring. Nowhere did this observer notice any discomfort; neither among teachers nor students.

The advisement period at the beginning of the school day is an efficient way to share information as to the activities of the school day. The sixth graders and the sixth grade teachers seemed to feel that they are very much a part of the school even though there are some differences in scheduling as compared to the other two grades. The program and the schedule seemed well-suited to the needs of the students.

If commendations were in order, they would be generously given.

I feel very good about the experience I had today. The teachers involved had no time to make special plans so I feel the day would be representative of a typical day.

A common element that was evident throughout the day was the positive upbeat attitude of students and teachers toward learning. Discipline problems in class were not evident in today's lessons.

The lessons were well organized and seemed to follow a sequential order. Students were involved in the learning and not just passive recipients of information. Also evident were the high expectations that teachers were setting for students. This was evident when teachers took time to explain not only the content of an assignment but also the format and level of quality necessary.

One teacher was trained in Hunters E^{3}1 program and was using active participation with her students.

In summary, I feel that I'm better able to promote public education in our middle school as a result of this very positive experience. *Kids are learning here* and there is no doubt in my mind about the high quality of education they are receiving.

Departmentalized Situations

As I sat in the sixth grade classrooms I realized what it was like to be a student again. The day seemed to move by very slowly and I became very restless.

It makes me realize how much time we expect a student to sit and listen in active learning. It became very tiring listening to an almost total teacher-directed class.

Overall the students seem to be learning but it made me question if we are teaching in the best possible way. I feel that the students need to be more actively involved. There should be more hands-on learning opposed to lecture and discussion. If lecture and discussion are used they should be in a more enthusiastic and creative manner, that keeps the interest of the students.

I believe we need to have our teachers go and be a student for a day to get their reaction to a day of school. I feel after a day of observation that teachers would become more aware of their expectations and hopefully question ways to improve.

The sixth graders and the student I was observing are continually involved in their classwork, and interacting with each other. They talk, and/or hurry no matter where they are going. Their day is busy with little time wasted. In fact, when a teacher stopped a few minutes early, even though I recognized that this was time wasted and not an effective teaching practice, I, along with the sixth graders, used the time to catch our breath. It was almost a welcome relief.

The pace was terrific—a lot of exciting things were taking place but, a lot of boring moments also. Most teachers exhibit some concern for the students, but a few were condescending, almost rude in some instances. All were organized for teaching the sixth graders, but only a few actually engaged in "reliable adult" roles or did not participate in school talk with the kids. The place where the kids find most caring, understanding, a mental relief to "study work," is in the gym. My student's gym teacher, along with the other coaches, demonstrated a sense of caring, humor, warmth, personal dignity, and instilled a keen desire to compete and excel. The coaches shared with the kids. They role modeled a reliable adult for the kids. The observer's student got into a situation of anger, frustration, and unsportsmanlike behavior. The coach, at the appropriate time (end of class), got him off to the side and talked to him, firmly, about his inappropriate behavior. It was well accepted and well done.

The experience of following a sixth grader the entire day provided me with some personal insight that few adults actually experience. The students were an energetic group with a healthy outlook on life. They were bright, concerned, and caring as they interacted with adults and fellow students.

It was a unique experience, with a unique student, and to me a very positive day. It gave me insight to what sixth graders do under various circumstances. They live for recognition and to be directed. I observed few discipline problems, a credit I gave to the sixth grade teachers.

There was a lot of variety in the lessons by the teachers and a spontaneous opportunity to learn came about in that one of the students found a dead snake and prepared the snake to be skinned at school. The teachers grouped and adapted a schedule to work the snake skinning that lasted about 30 minutes. A learning experience it was for me and the sixth graders were most appreciative. It helped me also to appreciate what they have to adapt to as seventh graders. The difference in the way students have to react to teachers and peers when they move up a grade is amazing.

The teachers emphasized a lot of responsibility to the students about looking after themselves. The kids right before lunch became quite restless. Lunch was very orderly, they marched to the serving line and sat at the same table for 25 minutes. The sixth graders were very comfortable at lunch and again highly regimented for control.

The sixth grader that I "shadowed" was structured from the start to the finish of the day. There were no big surprises for him to overcome. He was always thinking ahead for his next move, to avoid boredom I suppose. He was a leader with his 103 peers but he was not the strongest academically. He compensated through social skills. Other students looked to him as a leader outside the classroom but not in the classroom. He followed his agenda by thinking ahead as to what next. Sometimes so much that he was not paying attention to the present. Teacher did call on him and correct his answers. Overall he was one of the class and fit in well. An enlightened day for me indeed.

Most sixth grade students are still small and immature but are enjoying their new-found freedom—especially by March. They are eager to please and follow directions or guidance willingly. Their reactions to a particular class and/or teacher reflect their personal interest (or lack of interest) in the course as well as their relationship and rapport with the teacher. The classes with structure, change of pace and activity, involvement of students in the activities, recognition of individual contribution—were the ones where the students rebelled or "acted out" less. The teacher seemed to set the tone immediately!

The classroom environment made a tremendous difference, too. Physically, the room seemed to reflect the philosophy and personality of the teacher. Some rooms were comfortable and bright with the decor, work stations, seating arrangements set up to encourage immediate involvement and interaction between teacher and students. Others were dusty, noisy, cluttered, more rigidly arranged so that the students were removed from the teacher and interacted more among themselves. It was easy to project the ranking of favorite—least favorite classes and teachers of the student being observed.

Of most interest and/or concern to me was the student's reaction to the question about the person to whom he would turn if he were to need help on a personal problem. M. is a self-sufficient young man who worked harder in the classes that he liked, functioned better in the morning than the afternoon, "covered up" when he didn't know exactly what to do (e. g., computer class), and "doodled" when he was bored. He has perfected his own coping techniques for both classroom behavior and interpersonal relationships—whether in or out of the classroom. His teachers did vary in their willingness to focus on social or personal concerns with the majority being content-focused and one being totally discipline-focused.

CHAPTER 6

Summary, Conclusions, and Recommendations

T he effective, committed work of sixth grade teachers should not be over-looked or minimized. Critical analyses of the educational enterprise, such as the present study, must be viewed in the larger context and in full aware-ness of the positive aspects of the American educational enterprise. It is all too easy to analyze critically, failing to recognize the good that is inherent in all pub-lic education.

Yet, professional educators have a responsibility to pursue the improvement of education. Those of us at the middle level who are especially sensitive to the enduring importance of the educational experiences youth undergo during these developmental years feel a special responsibility.

This research study was not designed to be an exposé, another of those rhetorical reports which seem to appear with some regularity and delight in pointing the finger. Rather, it is an honest attempt, by practicing educators, to study the status of the sixth grade. It is based on the belief that this grade is in limbo, so to speak, and has not been specifically addressed. There have been inklings that all is not well in the sixth grade and that improvements are needed. This study, it is hoped, will help to focus attention on this important grade and lead to efforts that will make sixth grade education more effective in meeting the varied needs of these 11 and 12-year-old youths.

Upon reflection, we have to conclude that the shadow study data provided no real surprises, no truly unexpected conditions. In almost all respects, these data reaffirm the findings of earlier shadow studies and of other research proj-ects. The data support, too, what most anybody who is close to schools knows intuitively. Logic and one's cumulative experience in education would have led one to predict the nature of the findings. The fragmentation of the school day, the passive nature of so much schooling, the excessive sitting, the generally good behavior of pupils, the conscientiousness of teachers, the constant motion of early adolescents, all these conditions are well-known.

105

While the major weaknesses were predictable, so too were the positive conditions that make it clear that the basic elements and conditions needed for effective schools are in place. Teachers, with very limited exceptions, are conscientious and caring. Students are happy, and generally well-satisfied; they speak positively about their teachers, exhibit overall good behavior. Schools, though they vary in age and condition, almost always provide adequate physical facilities in which instruction can go on. Furniture and teaching materials are usually ample. Schools are well-organized and administered.

The above generalizations apply to other middle level grades as well as to the sixth grade. While lacks and gaps can quickly be identified and a wish list generated by any school, the more significant truth is that school improvement is really not held up by money or the things money can buy as much as it is by the attitudes of adults—teachers, administrators, board members, and parents—and by the perpetuation of old assumptions and traditions that are no longer valid.

Do Programs Match Developmental Realities?

The conflict between Mother Nature and the behavior and learning expectations of youth that are inherent in formal education is long-standing and, to some degree, inevitable. Mass education does involve some conformity, some imposition of adult judgments and standards—that is part of what youth is to learn. Yet, we know learning is most effective and efficient when its procedures and content are closely in tune with the nature and needs of the learner.

It is proper, therefore, to examine sixth grade programs in light of the realities of human growth and development. To what degree do programs reflect an awareness of the developmental needs and learning styles of 11 and 12-year-old young people? Do sixth grade programs assist youth as they face and move through the developmental processes associated with early adolescence? Are the known and applicable principles of learning reflected in the educational activities provided?

Questions such as these should be addressed. Even when theoretically correct solutions to the discrepancies noted are not easily attained or even attainable at all these matters still warrant serious consideration.

Chapter 2 provided an overview of sixth graders. The text identified many of the special characteristics of youngsters who are just moving into life's major period of growth and change. How do the programs revealed in the shadow studies match up with the profile of sixth graders presented in that chapter?

In the area of physical development there are clear discrepancies. Observers noted consistently the conflict between the physical need for movement and the sedentary nature of schooling. One analyst was "appalled" at the amount of sitting and said "I can't imagine how those squirrelly sixth graders could stand it." Another commented, "Sixth graders are required to sit for longer than we have a right to expect!" Almost without exception both observers and analysts commented in this vein. The growing bodies of 11 and 12-year-olds call for more opportunities for physical movement than schools currently provide.

Lacking more legitimate occasions for physical activity, sixth graders cross and uncross their legs constantly; they sit on their knees, they shift their positions every few minutes, they create reasons to get up and move around, they fidget.

Another major aspect of their physical development is, of course, sexual maturation. With limited exceptions, March 11, 1987, passed without the schools providing instruction or discussion on either the physical, social, or moral aspects of sex. If this, indeed, is the reality, it must be altered.

Nor was the tremendous variance in the level of maturation among sixth graders a factor in the activities planned for that day in March. It appeared as if a sixth grader was a sixth grader was a sixth grader irrespective of sex, height, weight, stage of development, or learning style. Individualization of instruction, so logical during this period of life, was sadly lacking, while whole class instruction predominated.

Milgram claims in Chapter 2 that "it is their developmental right to socialize, something they must learn how to do as one of the major tasks of adolescence." In this realm of development, young people are largely left to learn those lessons by independent study and trial and error. There were very few instances, indeed, that could be construed as attempts via the school program to give instruction or leadership in this area. Again, observers and analysts almost uniformly pointed out the very limited opportunities sixth graders are given to socialize, particularly in a learning context. The sixth graders, however, did exert their "right" and socialized incessantly. (One could only wish they were as adept in written language as they are in body language.)

Teachers did display sensitivity toward the emotional development of students. By providing individual help, recognizing individual differences, by touch, and by offering non-judgmental support the shadow studies revealed many, many sensitive, caring teachers were at work in our sixth grades. In departmentalized classes, however, these conditions were less evident than in self-contained rooms.

Where programs generally fell down was in the active promotion of opportunities for sixth graders to express their personal views, to try out various responses in order to judge peer and adult reactions, to experiment with ideas that involved feelings and judgments as well as information, to think critically.

It is generally recognized that a major aspect of adolescence is the generation of a unique identity by each individual. It is during the earliest stages of adolescence that young persons begin to initiate independent thought and activity, to see themselves as distinct persons, able to make decisions and judgments, to stand apart from their parents.

Schools traditionally have sought to contain rather than enhance this growing independence. And certainly the shadow studies provided evidence that this condition still prevails. Time after time observers and analysts decried the lack of involvement, the limited opportunities for independent action or judgment, and the infrequent give and take that leads to personal growth.

Milgram points out that "schools are capable of helping significantly or hindering seriously the development of sixth graders." This is indeed true and it lays a heavy responsibility on schools. While the shadow studies revealed only a very few instances of overt hindering they also included disappointingly few examples of ways sixth grade programs were helping in the overall development of students. A thoughtful review of learner characteristics and sixth grade programs as revealed in these studies reveals a mismatch on many points. There is a lack of congruity between much of what is done to and with sixth graders and their known nature and needs. This cannot be denied.

Where Should the Sixth Grade Be Located?

Where does the sixth grade belong? It depends on who you ask. Opinions vary. And so do relevant studies. The shadow study data do not show that sixth grades in elementary schools are providing better programs than sixth grades in middle schools—or worse programs. This is true whether you use an objective measurement (statistical analysis of checklists) or a subjective judgment based on reading and digesting the studies. Likewise, a tabulation of opinions expressed by observers reveals people on both sides of the question.

Among the views expressed by observers are these:

"After observing a sixth grade classroom for a day, I believe even more strongly that sixth graders belong in an elementary setting. The atmosphere was warm and caring and the teacher had the time to talk to students individually, working conferences in around other activities. Seventh graders seem more ready to attend a middle school or junior high. Even when courses are blocked at the middle level, teachers have far more students to work with and have less time to devote to each child."

_____

"After observing a sixth grade student, I feel that the concept of switching classes may be too much for some of these sixth graders. They have not yet developed any type of organization skills and it appears that it is being forced on them."

_____

"I would love to be a sixth grader in this particular self-contained class. The critical thinking skill of bi-directional analogies was fascinating especially when they drew their own to share with a partner.

"The day flowed well. The students moved easily from one activity to another. There was a sense that they were prepared for the upcoming content and/or activity. Expectations were clear.

"The students showed kindness and respect for the personal space of others. They functioned well at all times in the general space of the classroom."

_____

"I am convinced more than ever that sixth graders belong in a middle school environment.

"The physiological development of sixth graders is closer to the seventh grader. I noticed considerable physical differences between the sixth grader and the fifth grader. Naturally, these differences are also evident between sixth and seventh but they don't appear to be as great. Many of the boys and girls were as large as, if not larger than, my seventh graders.

"The need for physical activity is evident. The PE program available does not meet the needs of the students. The students were restless and up and around the class frequently.

"Sixth graders need variety. Elementary staffs and schools, for the most part, are not equipped or trained to meet the exploratory needs of sixth graders.

"Sixth graders need strict teachers. They need a set of rules to abide by and a teacher who enforces the rules. This class was very responsive to assertive discipline.

"The unique needs of sixth graders call for a lot of counseling time. The ratio here was about 1-800, far too large to be effective."

"From my experience and my observations, I conclude that the sixth graders do fit well enough into the middle school atmosphere, as long as there are some modifications to fit their developmental stage. For example, I disagree with this school's policy of permitting sixth graders to attend school dances; they are sorely lost and out of place in such a setting. But sixth grade is a level—no matter where the students are housed—in which competency concentrations must not be sacrificed for the sake of a 'secondary' type atmosphere, or for any other reason, in my view."

"After observing a self-contained sixth grade for a day, I wonder if the students found the day lacking in variety as much as I did. It reinforced my idea that the teacher's personality is the key to what happens in the classroom. The room I observed was very well organized and quiet. Everyone seemed to know what assignments were due. There was no large group presentation or discussion. My student managed to add variety and social interaction to his day, however. I was concerned with the apparently small amount of time spent on tasks. This day reinforces the need for a middle school."

"Sixth graders are a unique, interesting, complex age. We used to have them in the middle school. We were then comprised of 6-8, but returned them to the elementary school after a few years. I was opposed to the move then, and I still believe they belong in the middle school setting. Watching them for this study has made me equally firm in that conviction. Girls, especially, are so much more like middle schoolers than elementary kids, and have needs for activities, challenges, and individualized attention that are so much more easily met in the middle school setting. There was a great deal of social behavior observed by me, but seemingly ignored by the classroom teacher which is typical of young adolescents and more easily tolerated by personnel who are attuned to the physical and emotional needs of middle schoolers.

"Observing the physical restlessness and the behaviors between sexes further convinced me that this age group belongs with older kids. I think the inattention and short attention spans showed that the kids cannot handle the self-contained environment. They need movement and change at shorter intervals, and daily PE activities. They also demonstrated in their music and computer classes a need for and a high interest in 'elective' or 'exploratory' areas which are not as readily available to them in the elementary school setting."

It is clear that there are advantages that accrue to a sixth grade located in an elementary school which still follows a predominately self-contained approach. More personal attention, less stress, and more interrelated instruction are examples of likely results. On the other hand, a middle level school with more of a secondary approach would probably provide more exploratory experiences, greater variety in approaches, and more ample instructional and physical resources.

Each type of school has advantages and disadvantages. The answer to the question, "Where does the sixth grade belong?" is not to be found in the administrative unit that houses it. Many other factors must be considered—the nature of the school program above and below, school size, the competence and attitudes of faculty, for instance. The key question to ask is, "Where can sixth graders' educational *and* developmental needs best be met given the conditions prevailing in the local situation?"

Final Conclusions and Recommendations

Many conclusions with related recommendations often inherent in them have been presented earlier in this chapter and in Chapter 3. Chapter 4 closes with a number of conclusions growing out of the detailed checklist data analysis. These judgments closely parallel those derived from the study of the shadow studies themselves as presented in Chapter 5. The concluding statements to follow are mutually supported by both types of data. It is hoped that these affirmations will point to needed improvements.

1. There is no justification for choosing to use full departmentalization in the sixth grade. There may be situations where conditions do not seem to permit an immediate choice. The preparation of the faculty and/or the faculty's mental health may seem to rule in favor of utilizing departmentalization in the sixth grade. In such situations, departmentalization should be openly acknowledged as the temporary arrangement and specific plans, including related staff development activities, should be initiated for moving away from departmentalization.

The clear conflict between the developmental needs of sixth graders and the fragmented, subject-centered departmentalized day must be acknowledged and incorporated into program improvement plans. The content dealt with at this grade level simply does not require the level of sophistication and expertise found in the single subject specialist; whereas the critical importance of their developmental needs calls for a smaller number of teachers who know them well and have some contact with them beyond a single period. Educators probably have not been sufficiently conscious of what is given up when organizing to provide separate subject specialists. Losses, while subtle, probably outweigh the presumed benefit of expertise in subject matter, especially for sixth graders.

2. On the other hand, it seems equally clear that a purely self-contained, elementary oriented sixth grade is no more appropriate for *emerging* adolescents. The social and exploratory needs of early adolescents are not likely to be met adequately when only a single teacher directs the entire day save for, perhaps, art and music. Eleven and 12-year-olds are emerging from childhood and are seeking understanding and experiences beyond the limited scope of the usual self-contained classroom. Their need for exploratory experiences is impelling. While a single teacher may be able to provide much of the variety needed there has to be a context and support for so doing that is not normally found in an elementary school.

3. In order to serve its role as a transition school a middle level institution should organize the sixth grade in a manner that is different from the fifth grade but certainly not just as the seventh grade is organized. A two person team for the basic academics or a three subject core block with one primary teacher, for instance, are appropriate ways of organizing a sixth grade. The shadow studies make evident the potential value of teaming in offsetting the effects of "bigness." Middle level schools tend to be fairly large which may make curriculum options greater, but also produces stress for younger students and leads to the anonymity that plagues so much of contemporary education.

4. In order to provide the needed climate, context, and curriculum for early adolescents continued efforts should be made to establish a distinctive middle level. This level, which usually includes the sixth grade along with the seventh and eighth grades, encompasses the greatest percentage of students who are in the transition period between childhood and full adolescence. Programs directed to the needs of these changing young people would, therefore, be more likely to develop.

There are many subtle conditions and assumptions present in a school that considers itself elementary or secondary. Without being called up for examination or reconsideration these factors nevertheless underlie many administrative, curriculum, and instructional decisions. Both sets of conditions and assumptions have validity when applied to the general population of elementary or secondary education—but neither is really valid when applied to those who are enrolled in the sixth grade. As persons "in transition" the educational experiences of these students, as well as those in the seventh and eighth grades, need to be directed by assumptions that apply specifically to them. Their diversity must be recognized. The rate of the changes that are taking place must also be taken into account. Sixth graders in September are quite different from sixth graders in May.

5. Strong efforts to actually implement interdisciplinary instruction and realize its potential must be put forth. The continued fragmentation of learning, even in situations where teachers are organized as teams, retards achievement as well as other aspects of development. In fact, one of the major disappointments in the study was discovering how little correlation and fusion exists in schools claiming to be practicing interdisciplinary planning and teaching.

6. The strong socialization drive of sixth grade students should be utilized positively in the pursuit of academic learning. Cooperative learning, peer teaching, and other techniques that do this have been shown to be effective in enhancing achievement. The use of such approaches should be implemented.

7. Sixth grade students who are reaching for independence should be given increased opportunities to make decisions and participate actively in the teaching-learning process. The high degree of passive, exclusively teacher directed learning now found in sixth grades is not defensible. A higher level of intellectualization should be encouraged along with this involvement.

8. The guidance services available to most sixth graders are woefully inadequate. The excessively high student-counselor ratios, which averaged more than 400 to 1, all but eliminate the opportunity for counselors to do much preventive group guidance and confer regularly with classroom teachers. When no teacher-based guidance program, such as an adviser-advisee arrangement, is in place, it is almost certain that the varied developmental, social, and personal concerns of these emerging adolescents will go unattended by school personnel. Sixth graders need an understanding adult advocate as they move into a multi-teacher day and such a person may or may not emerge and be available when needed.

9. Period length, whether 45, 50, or 55 minutes, does not match the attention span of sixth graders or recognize their physical development. Conscientious efforts should be made by teachers to provide varied, hands-on activities, changes of pace, and opportunities for physical movement. Such activities should also incorporate opportunities for interaction between students and between students and teachers.

The Big Truth

Out of this study, as in the comparable studies previously conducted of the seventh, eighth, and ninth grades, comes one major truth, a truth so central to improvement efforts that it must not be by-passed. *The teacher makes the difference.* It is not school unit, grade organization, interdisciplinary teaming, relevant curriculum content, or anything else, that is *the* essential factor in the improvement of middle level education. It is the quality of the classroom teacher.

Differences in the shadow study data that could be attributed solely to school locale or to instructional organization were surprisingly small. Teamed situations, though having much greater potential, were not automatically better. The self-contained classroom, when in the hands of an excellent teacher, may have some advantages for sixth graders.

Teachers, inevitably, hold the trump cards and the opportunity to play them as they will. To improve sixth grade programs staff development efforts must be so designed that teachers will grow in their understanding, attitudes, and self-concepts. Some efforts, of course, must also be directed to developing improved administrative procedures, establishing common planning periods, securing more adequate instructional resources and other needed supportive factors, but without giving attention to teacher growth these other improvements will have little lasting effect.

A Final Word

The sixth grade is a nice place for youngsters to be. Life there, whatever its failings may be, is pretty exciting. The curiosity of sixth graders is heightened; new interests are emerging. Major physical changes are already evident or eagerly anticipated. Socialization is becoming an all-engrossing facet of life and to be among one's peers at such a time is "duck soup." Risks, at this level, are limited and behavior, though increasingly exuberant, is somewhat restrained.

For teachers as well as students the sixth grade has much to commend it. Sixth graders have high regard and appreciation for their teachers. They express pride in their schools.

Improving sixth grade education is, then, not a hopeless task of countering deep-seated and negative views. Existing conditions provide a solid foundation. Teachers are conscientious and caring. Schools are effectively administered. Available materials are sufficient. No revolution is called for or needed. Yet, there are shortcomings evident and obvious student needs that should be addressed. We hope this study of the sixth grade will provide guidance for efforts to make life in the sixth grade even better.

The reactions and comments of one observer (based on Shadow Study Number 5, page 69), are so well-articulated, perceptive, and challenging that they warrant inclusion here as the concluding words of this study.

An Observer's Reactions

(Written in my car parked at a shopping mall spontaneously, right after leaving the school of my Shadow Study.)

How fortunate I am to have randomly found Glorianne!
   I believe that today was a contribution
    to another step in her adjustment as a transescent.
One teacher said she lived with a grandmother;
   hinted at a broken home.
    - From Glorianne, I learned that her father had died
    and her mother moved here from a small town (2,000)
    to be near her family in this suburban city.
Later today, teachers called her their "success story",
   saying she had cried every day, last fall at beginning,
   and had stomach aches. They had told her to sit
   with other students, not alone.
    —She no longer cries — at school. She has learned
     how to sit alone.
My heart aches for her.
   Her teachers don't really know her nor her story.
    —She is a courageous girl who will make it,
     perhaps in spite of school, not because of it.

What schools do to kids!
   I saw, today, through the eyes of one sixth-grader.

Physically:

Glorianne is tiny. Her feet cannot reach the floor from
   any student chair.
   How would you feel, if your feet always dangled?
   No wonder she sat on her legs and feet
    or perched on her knees, at her desk.
There was no chance to go to the rest room.
   How _could_ you, with 3 minutes to rush between
    classes, often with a locker stop for gym suit, lunch,
    or art work?
   How could you make it to the far end of the hall,
    not even in your sixth grade area, and
    way beyond the intimidating, adult-filled offices?
   Who would risk embarrassment of asking
    a strict teacher for a pass, in front of peers,
    in the middle of a class?
    —"You learn to live with it," as some girls said.
    Glorianne's plan was to go the last minute
    at home before school, and not drink anything.
There was little opportunity to move around
   in the classrooms. Students sat in rows of seats,
   mostly, obediently, quietly.

Emotionally:

As I observed Glorianne, I wondered—
   How do you feel when you can't make friends?
   When you're not allowed to talk in class;
    when the desirable behavior is silent,
    solitary desk work;
   When there are no opportunities to work
    purposefully with others; I saw no group work;
   When the objective even in Phys. Ed. is to
    win points and not play with people
   When teachers expect silence and rote answers
    and paper work;
   When you're thrown in with "not nice" peers,
    as Glorianne said;
   When teachers are remote and
    aren't even sincerely friendly;

when even fun things are organized by adults
   and become not-fun;
when there are no advisor/advisee groups or
   opportunities to know and care and share with
   other kids and possibly one significant adult?
Teachers seemed to become strict in the classroom.
   How do students feel and respond
   in such a relationship?
   I saw only one teacher who -
      praised Glorianne and commented publicly
         on her notebook,
      admitted he made a mistake today AND last week,
      spontaneously threw in advice (on neatness) and values,
      related to where his class kids are, and
      used names in personalized encouragement.
   The rest -
      had rules and piles of paperwork to push,
      got uptight over a bit of conversation
      or busy-work hum, and
      didn't smile.

Educationally:

Glorianne was kept busy all day with
   dittoed sheets to fill in the answers
      (even in art class),
   reading the text book and writing the answers,
   orally answering fact questions.
Not once was she challenged to have
   an original thought.
Teachers would walk and talk and tell;
   Students were to sit and listen and remember.
Desks were lined up
   facing the lecturing authority;
Teachers did not respect the silence they asked
   their students to keep;
   they walked noisily, talked aloud, interrupted.
...Etc.... but I was not there to evaluate teachers,
   only to observe how they affected Glorianne.

Environmentally:

Room arrangements seemed either
   unplanned or for teacher convenience.
   I had a strong feeling of uncomfortableness
   as I imagined myself
   sitting where Glorianna had to sit -
      back to natural light,
      crowded toward uninspiring, cramped
         front of room,
      rows and not groups or interest centers,
      assigned seats in every case, I guessed.
Bulletin boards were teacher-made,
   no obvious student involvement or choices.
Rules, made by adults, were prominently posted.
Rooms were dreary, with non-creative contents,
   dull colors.
Halls were institutionally plain, lined with lockers.
Too many people were moving at once.
Bells rang for class changes.
   Teams were clustered; it would seem
      they could have moved without bells.
   Students were penalized
      if they were late (sentence writing,
      more work, themes...)
      Fear was evident.
Public address system was distracting.
   Poor mechanical reception - and delivery-
      of announcements.
   Interruptions were of questionable importance.

Structurally - Schedule:

Lunch restrictions, regimentation, regulations
    appeared to be more important than relationships.
Why did sixth graders (youngest) eat last (12:30-1)?

Conceptually:

If this be a middle school,
    where were middle school concepts used?
What joy is there for Glorianne
    who can't make friends in a new school
        because you can't talk;
    who has all the talking and deciding
        done for her by teachers;
    who is pressured to go here...,
        finish paper...;
    whose learning is not made relevant
        nor adventurous;
    who is not much treated like a person,
        much less a kid of 6th grade age;
    who experiences learning
        under harried adults
        ("I like teaching kids; I don't like my job")
        who have taken on the pressure of
        "maintaining control" lest all be lost!
They _said_ the team was all in one area,
    but there were long walks,
        under time pressure
        in crowded halls of 6th, 7th and 8th graders.
There were few or no choices 'by 'student input.
    Glorianne intuitively recognized this by saying
        that any choices she might have are "dead-end."
High school methods were frequently used—
        for sixth-grade Glorianne!
    Class changes by the bell/clock.
    Specialized teachers by subject.
    Student mixes
        Too much mixing. For pupils' good or
            for discipline ease?
        There seemed no opportunity for
            group building; in fact there was an
            opposite attempt to keep control
            by isolation or separation of friends.
    Class seating seemed planned by
        the teacher to build barriers to talk.
    Lecture. Listen. Recite. Read. Write.
        No group work, no student "contests",
            nor learning games, etc.
    Lack of privacy in locker room.
        Change of clothes was in one, large,
            public area; no privacy for growing girls.
"International Day" was to occur during Reading class
    the next day. It seemed an opportunity
    for interdisciplinary learning, but the only
    cooperation obvious was by the teachers
    allowing rehearsal during the last period,
    when they collectively provided "discipline".
"Team planning" was referred to,
    but I did not see results,
    as there was no great rapport among teachers
    and no obvious benefit to Glorianne
    except organization
    to tell students what, where, when, how.
        Glorianne remarked about liking the
        organization at the beginning of the
        school year; but by now (March)
        her need is to move from security
        to involved responsibility.

116

Conclusion:

I really feel quite angry that we cannot seem able to make schools places of joyous learning for students who are naturally eager for experiences in learning and in relationships. Instead, we give them regimented, routine repetition of busy work on dull fact finding, in isolated, unenforcible silence.

Why can't we —
  be more aware
    of students' feelings and point of view;
  be creative enough
        to find solutions
            even in old buildings,
              despite limited funds,
                with tired teachers
                    wanting revitalization;
    be open
      to fresh insights,
      to possibilities and alternatives,
        in spite of out-moded tradition ?
Why can't we, across America —
  construct school buildings
      of beauty and color and comfort;
  find teachers
      who love kids
          as persons of worth, like themselves;
      who continue to grow and to polish skills;
      who come to class
            with enthusiasm and ideas
          to provide happy experiences
          and mutually-shared learning
              for both kids and teachers ?
Who can start the ball rolling
    toward wide-spread, sweeping changes
    to make learning for all the Gloriannes —
                  and their teachers —
      more of an adventure
          than a battle or endurance race ?

It puzzles me —
  that this school is reputed to be a "good" school.
      People visit it
          and are proudly shown around.
    They are pleased they sent a team
          to present at a middle school conference.
    The staff were well-informed and well-intentioned;
          the words sounded right in the office.
    The schedule appeared adequate, on paper.
  that the teachers,
        in talking to me and to each other,
    seemed like ordinary people —
        good, polite, conversant, able to laugh, human —
    but in front of their classes
        they somehow became
              forcibly nice,
              shrill-voiced,
              excessively controlling,
              tense under pressure,
              accusatory of a slight infraction
                      of their rules,
            and oblivious to
                  students' needs and wants,
                  raised hands,
                  and relevancy.
  Only one of Glorianne's teachers
        seemed tuned-in to kids,
      and he expressed feelings of being caught
          in a frustrating system.

117

I am afraid
  that this school and anonymous others
    would be on the defensive
      if they picked themselves out in this study;
  that they expect and will look for
    a glowing report of the wonderful things
      resulting from what they are doing.

And I feel apologetic.
  I know that much good is in this school.

But today
  I saw through the eyes of a sixth grade student.
  I ran her race through a day in time.
  I felt her concerns and fears and joys,
  I empathized with her smiles and tears
      (of which there were both).
  I understood her anxieties and boredom
      and sheer happiness.
  I peered beneath her conforming exterior
      to her inner quest for love.

Therefore, I feel involved as an advocate,
      albeit frustratingly helpless,
  and I must express my concerns.

I would like to find answers
  to my own doubts and disappointment
      over what I saw today
        from Glorianne's perspective,
    climaxed by her discovery
        of her special-ness in this study
      with her response of utter happiness,
        joy, and come-alive hope,
  and I share that hope.

Schools have a tremendous, complex task.
  Administrators and teachers
      usually work very hard.
  Community and parent expectations
    are high and demanding.
  Teachers, by and large, like people. Some like kids.
  As a cross-section,
      perhaps not many are creative,
    and if a few are,
        they dare not rock the boat, be different.
  Safety lies in conformity.
      So, we teach the safe way —
        orderly, organized, ordinary.

Change is difficult and slow,
      because we deal with people,
          the system is ingrained,
          tradition is strong.

Any widespread change in our nation's schools
        for the benefit of all Gloriannes
    must be a concerted effort
      by the most creative,
              visionary,
                experienced
        leaders of national repute,
    implemented by
        responsive, enthusiastic, intelligent,
          caring, capable teachers in the classrooms
      and understanding administrators
        who know what it's like
          for the students "out there".

These comments
    are jotted down (and not edited)
        as an attempt
            to deal with my feelings,
            to organize my thoughts
                    about today's experience,
            and to seek to understand
                how we might become
                    more effective educators
            for the children in our care
                and
            for the only sure
                and hopeful fact of life —
                        change.

I must give credit
    that we have a public school system
        where committed, capable teachers
            daily give of themselves in great measure,
        where knowledge is abundantly available,
        where wonderful adults do serve kids;
    that I was privileged today
            to visit one of these public schools
        which are striving to do the best they can
            for Glorianne
            and all the other Gloriannes
            and Shauns and Marias and Miquels
            and your children and our grandchildren
            and our country's citizens and leaders
            and teachers
                    of tomorrow.

My question to you who read this report:
    —What can you do
        to act upon the compiled findings
            of this Shadow Study?

    —What are you going to do?

Related Research Studies

While this monograph was designed only to report on the Sixth Grade Project, three related research studies are of such importance that they should be cited. Educators anxious to acquire a full understanding of problems relating to grade placement, organizational options, and instructional procedures will want to become familiar with these major studies, all of which have clear implications for middle level education.

1. Simmons, Roberta G., and Blyth, Dale A. *Moving into Adolescence: The Impact of Pubertal Change and School Context.* New York: Aldine de Gruyter, 1987.

A major, long-term (5 year) scientific study that investigated the impact of age, gender, pubertal timing, and timing of school transition on the self-image and social-psychological adjustment of white youth. It compared the effects of a self-contained organization with those of a departmentalized one.

The findings are extensive and detailed. In general, the study reveals some long-lasting disadvantages of the junior high school, especially for girls. Entry into a middle school at grade 5 or 6 would predate much of adolescence and thus would engender less stress. The importance of schools providing an "arena of comfort" and countering the impersonality of large schools is made clear. The real effects of "top dog" and "bottom dog" status are discussed along with many other aspects of the relationship between pubertal change and schools.

2. Center for Research on Elementary and Middle Schools. *Special Report on Middle School.* Baltimore, Md.: The Johns Hopkins University, CREMS Report, June 1987.

This report, "A Description of Organizational Structure in Middle Schools and Their Effects on Student-Teacher Relations and Instruction," summarizes three of the research studies accomplished by the associates of program director, Joyce Epstein. (The three reports are available from the Center as Reports 14, 15, and 16, all dated June 1987.)

The first study describes the practices currently existing in staffing, grouping, and scheduling. The shadow study data confirm the more comprehensive findings of this study. The issue of departmentalization versus self-contained classrooms is analyzed thoroughly in the second study. The more positive student-teacher relationship evident in self-contained classrooms was weighed against the presumed higher quality instruction in departmentalized situations. The third study examines the effects of departmentalization, tracking, and within-class ability grouping on the achievement of four groups of students based on socioeconomic status. Generally, it appears that departmentalization favors only the higher level students.

3. Eccles, Jacqueline, and Associates. Ann Arbor, Mich.: University of Michigan, Institute for Social Research.

Utilizing grants from several sources, the Institute for Social Research at the University of Michigan conducted a number of comprehensive studies on early adolescent development and person-environment fit. Taken together the studies indicate that classrooms are not optimally responsive to the developmental needs of early adolescents.

Among findings are these: junior high schools stifle creativity and injure self-esteem. Elementary students have more opportunity to express their opinions and make decisions than do junior high students despite the known increased need for such by early adolescents. Post-transition (junior high) teachers trust students less, emphasize discipline more, and have a lower sense of efficacy than do pre-transition (elementary) teachers.

The Shadow Study Technique

The Shadow Study Technique, a quasi-ethnographic procedure, supplies realistic snapshots of the educational experiences individuals undergo during an actual school day. By focusing on a randomly selected pupil and the minute-by-minute activities and actions of that pupil a revealing picture of the educational process is presented. Although the actions of teachers are very much a part of that picture, by looking at the day's events through the eyes of a pupil a different and in many ways a more valid perspective is secured than when focusing on the teacher's activities. When taken together and analyzed these shadow studies provide a dramatic picture of the real curriculum, the curriculum actually experienced by the individual pupil.

This research procedure has been used previously in conducting studies of middle level grades (Lounsbury and Johnston, 1985; Lounsbury, Marani, and Compton, 1980; Lounsbury and Marani, 1964). It has also been used by many individual schools and hundreds of preservice teachers as an effective way to get close to the reality of organized education.

The value of this exercise to the individual observer is notable apart from any other use made of the data gathered. Observers in this study, for instance, volunteered these assessments:

"Observing a sixth grader every period of the day including the lunch period was very rewarding . . . It was an opportunity entirely different from what we are used to in administration in which we concentrate more on the interaction between teachers and the class as a whole."

"What an experience! Having spent a day observing a sixth grader and minimally interacting with the teachers and staff, I discovered that the experience was professionally rewarding and it gave me a better sense of appreciation of what life was like when I vicariously tried to live the school day as the student experienced it."

"First and foremost, it is recommended that school personnel with non-classroom assignments do this type of study. The insights and feelings of what middle school is really about would surely influence decision making and attitudes."

"I suggest that every teacher take time out to 'walk in the shoes' of the students. The results would probably be revolutionary."

While recognizing the value of the experience almost as universal a comment deals with its demands. These sixth grade observer remarks are typical:

122

"I am *tired*."

"One thing I know after this activity is that this sixth grader should have been tired at the end of a very full day—almost no time to relax and take a break —his observer was!"

"The opportunity to shadow a sixth grade student was an exciting, though exhausting experience for me. By the end of the day, I was ready to go and 'crash'."

The procedures for conducting a study are outlined in the sheet, "Directions for Observers," which was used in this project and is reproduced below. The form use to collect the data is simply an 8 1/2 by 11" sheet turned lengthwise and divided into four columns as indicated here:

Study Observation Form

Time	Specific behavior at 5-7 minute intervals	Environment	Impression-Comments

Directions for Observers

In March, 1987, you will be engaging in an important research study. As one of the many volunteer observers from across the country, you will follow a randomly selected sixth grade student, and, as nearly as possible, live the school day as he or she does, recording events and impressions. This day will prove to be a valuable, informative, and meaningful experience for you personally. It will also provide the raw data needed to seek answers to questions concerning the sixth grade.

To ensure reasonable objectivity, uniformity, and success, please read the following directions and follow them carefully.

1. Make prior arrangements with the school to be visited. It is important that teachers understand the purpose of your visit and know that you are not evaluating them or the school.

2. Clear your calendar for March 11 so that you will be free the entire day to complete the shadow study.

3. Arrive at the school 15 minutes or so ahead of the school opening. Secure or arrange for securing, the basic data called for on the cover sheet provided. (This may well be done at the end of the day.)

4. Select a sixth grade student using a technique that will ensure randomness. *Please do not let school personnel select a "good" student for you.* Means of ensuring randomness include:

   (a) Ask someone to pick a number between 1 and 25. On the roster of sixth grade students whose last name begins with your middle initial, select that numbered student.

   (b) Locate the file drawer of sixth grade student folders and pick, blindly, a folder. (*Note*: If the student selected is in a special education class for more than 25 percent of the day, pick another student.)

5. Locate the selected student's homeroom (or first period) and, with the help of the teacher, unobtrusively identify the student to be shadowed. Find a seat out of the way and look as nonchalant as possible.

6. Using the forms provided, record the information desired. While you can't be oblivious to other matters, try to keep your focus on the individual student and what he or she is apparently doing. (Use an initial or fictitious name for student shadowed.)

7. The 5-7 minute time interval will give you a bit of flexibility, but will definitely show the flow of actions and activities. Start a new time interval with each change of class or period. Go with the student to gym, lunch, and, as nearly as possible, keep up with the individual so you can experience vicariously his or her full school day.

8. If the student, after the third or fourth hour, confronts you with the question, "Are you following me?" pass it off with a vague statement such as, "You know, I guess you have been in every class I've visited." In this and all cases, your intuition and common sense will be the best guide.

9. At the close of the last period (or close to it, if you've cleared with the teacher), pull the student aside for an interview. (See separate sheet for details on interview and list of questions.) You may want to tape record the interview.

10. Check out with the office, secure information needed to complete general information sheet, and express appreciation.

11. Open the sealed envelope and complete the "Program Characteristics or Conditions" sheet.

12. That evening, if at all possible, write out your impressions, reactions, and conclusions while the day's events are still fresh in your mind.

13. Have the original shadow study typed onto fresh forms to ensure readability. Please include your name (as you would like it to appear in the final report), professional address, and telephone number.

14. Mail the typed study, the interview, the general data sheet, and your personal reflections within *10 days* to:

    National Association of Secondary School Principals
    1904 Association Drive
    Reston, Virginia 22091
    Attention: George E. Melton

References

Lounsbury, J. H., and Johnston, J. H. *How Fares the Ninth Grade?* Reston, Va.: National Association of Secondary School Principals, 1985.

Lounsbury, J. H.; Marani, J.; and Compton, M. *The Middle School in Profile: A Day in the Seventh Grade*. Columbus, Ohio: National Middle School Association, 1980.

Lounsbury, J. H., and Marani, J. *The Junior High School We Saw: One Day in the Eighth Grade*. Alexandria, Va..: Association for Supervision and Curriculum Development, 1964.

Observers Who Conducted Shadow Studies

ANN AMICARELLI
Cumberland Middle School
Cumberland, R.I.

THOMAS AMOS
Central School
Glencoe, Ill.

MARIE MOREY ANGAIAK
Anchorage School District
Anchorage, Alaska

STANLEY ANGELL
E. G. Kromrey Middle School
Middleton, Wis.

NELSON ARMOUR
Central School
Glencoe, Ill.

GWYNE ARNOLD
Mills E. Godwin Middle School
Woodbridge, Va.

NORMA RAE ARRINGTON
Retired Educator
Provo, Utah

SIDNEY BAILEY
Westwood Middle School
Grand Rapids, Mich.

REX O. BARNES
Quincy Junior High School
Quincy, Ill.

EDWARD A. BARNHART
Sterling Middle School
East Wenatchee, Wash.

JAN BARTON
Parent Volunteer
Southmayd, Tex.

VAUGHN BELCHER
Alcoa Middle School
Alcoa, Tenn.

PAUL BELOBRAJDIC
Jonathan Turner Junior High School
Jacksonville, Ill.

ROY C. BENAVIDES
W. W. Jackson Middle School
San Antonio, Tex.

JOAN M. BLOOMER
Prince Willliam County Public Schools
Manassas, Va.

DOUGLAS J. BOHRER
Wall Intermediate School
Wall, N.J.

GARY BOLTON
Fremont Junior High School
Fremont, Nebr.

NEILA A. CONNORS
Valdosta State College
Valdosta, Ga.

RON BOMMERSBACH
Prairie View Elementary School
Devils Lake, N.Dak.

JOHN A. CORKERY
Linn-Mar Junior High School
Marion, Iowa

KATHY BONE
Omak Middle School
Omak, Wash.

DEE CRAMER
Ysleta Independent School District
El Paso, Tex.

CATHERINE BOOKER
Browne Junior High School
Washington, D.C.

LEANN CROWLEY
Knox County Schools
Knoxville, Tenn.

KATHLEEN A. BRENNAN
Wall Intermediate School
Wall, N.J.

JEANNE L. DARROW
Social Worker
Powell, Wyo.

ROBERT BRUCE
Union Park Junior High School
Orlando, Fla.

DAVID DELANEY
Lincoln Elementary School
Jamestown, N.Dak.

EDDIE BUTLER
Booker T. Washington Middle School
Mobile, Ala.

NANCY DOLAN
Horizon Middle School
Aurora, Colo.

DOUGLAS BYINGTON
O'Brien Middle School
Reno, Nev.

RICHARD DORMUTH
Pembrook Middle School
North Wales, Penn.

JULIA CAMPBELL
McKinley Junior High School
Cedar Rapids, Iowa

JAMES DYER
Alta Loma Junior High School
Alta Loma, Calif.

WILLIAM CANTER
Roosevelt Junior High School
Newark, Ohio

CORWIN ELLSWORTH
Supai Middle School
Scottsdale, Ariz.

CHRISTINE CARAM
Country Estates Elementary School
Midwest City, Okla.

ROGER EPPERLY
Del Crest Heights Junior High School
Del City, Okla.

CLAIRE COLE
Montgomery County Public Schools
Christiansburg, Va.

DONNA ERIKSON
Falmouth Middle School
Falmouth, Maine

ANNE MARIE COLLINS
Gresham School District
Gresham, Oreg.

DEBBIE ESTES
S & S Middle School
Southmayd, Tex.

KEVIN FENNELL
Harvest Park Middle School
Pleasanton, Calif.

ANNE FLETCHER
West Georgia R.E.S.A.
Grantville, Ga.

HAROLD GOLDBERG
Clark Lane Junior High School
Waterford, Conn.

JAMES P. HAESSLY
School District of Waukesha
Waukesha, Wis.

RICHARD HAGEN
Waunakee Middle School
Waunakee, Wis.

LORETTA HARPER
Walker-Grant Intermediate School
Fredericksburg, Va.

KENT M. HARRIS
Lamar Middle School
Lamar, Mo.

MICHAEL J. HERMANS
Edison Middle School
Green Bay, Wis.

PATRICIA HO
Kawananakoa Intermediate School
Honolulu, Hawaii

DIANE HONESH
Garden City Junior High School
Garden City, N.J.

JEAN A. HUBBARD
Powell Middle School
Powell, Wyo.

MARY HURLEY
Parent Volunteer
Munster, Ind.

JANICE HYDE
DeRidder Junior High School
DeRidder, La.

BEVERLY J. IRWIN
Parent Volunteer
Verona, Wis.

PAULA JACK-FIX
5 Oaks Intermediate School
Beaverton, Oreg.

PEP JEWELL
Havre Junior High School
Havre, Mont.

PATT KAMM
Lewis-Palmer Middle School
Monument, Colo.

DEBBY KASAK
Jefferson Middle School
Champaign, Ill.

SUZANNE E. KAUNITZ
Hoover Middle School
Kenmore, N.Y.

GERALD KEITH
Carthage Junior High School
Carthage, Mo.

IRENE J. KENT
Hoover Middle School
Kenmore, N.Y.

GEORGINE KEROACK
Parent Volunteer
Gilford, N.H.

GERALDINE KIESSEL
Garden City Junior High School
Garden City, Mich.

VICKIE KIVELL
Story Elementary School
Allen, Tex.

JUDITH LADD
Woodbridge Middle School
Woodbridge, Va.

CHARLES LANG
Hillsdale Middle School
Mobile, Ala.

CECIL ANN LEARY
McCulloch Middle School
Dallas, Tex.

ALPHONSE LEWIS
Waco Independent School District
Waco, Tex.

DAN LONG
Cedar Rapids Schools
Cedar Rapids, Iowa

BONITA I. LYNCH
El Dorado Middle School
El Dorado, Kans.

EDMUND R. MAHONEY
Ottoson Junior High School
Arlington, Mass.

MELDINE L. MALONEY
Rosemont Middle School
Norfolk, Va.

GLENN MAYNARD
Kent State University
Kent, Ohio

MARION MCCALLISTER
Suzanne Middle School
Walnut, Calif.

JUDY MCCUTCHEN
Sterling Middle School
East Wenatchee, Wash.

ROBIN MCDONALD
Walnut Springs Middle School
Westerville, Ohio

NITA MCEACHERN
Towanda Elementary School
Towanda, Kans.

BETTY MCKEE
North Omak Elementary School
Omak, Wash.

BETTY MELTON
Coral Springs Middle School
Coral Springs, Fla.

JOSEPH MEYSKENS
Bothwell Middle School
Marquette, Mich.

MARY MILLAR
Harvest Park Middle School
Pleasanton, Calif.

WILLIAM J. MORKRID
Wayzata West Junior High School
Wayzata, Minn.

MARTHA NAGELE
Substitute Teacher
Westlake, Ohio

DEBORAH A. NOENNICH
New Castle Middle School
New Castle, Del.

PATRICK V. NOLAN
Linn-Mar Junior High School
Marion, Iowa

JOHN H. NORMAN
Ryan Middle School
Fairbanks, Alaska

PATRICIA A. OLSEN
Bothwell PTO
Marquette, Mich.

KATIE O'ROURKE
Ladera del Norte Elementary School
Farmington, N. Mex.

DEBRA PAVIGNANO
Chatham Middle School
Chatham, N.J.

JOHN A. POHL
Holman Middle School
St. Ann, Mo.

BOBBIE POOLE
University of N. Colorado
    Laboratory Middle School
Greeley, Colo.

KATHRYN T. POWELL
Georgia College
Milledgeville, Ga.

THOMAS QUINNERY
Gilford Middle School/High School
Gilford, N.H.

JOE RAMIREZ
South Junior High School
Edinburg, Tex.

MARTHA K. RANEY
Hubbard Middle School
Tyler, Tex.

HOWARD F. RASH
Northwest Middle School
Knoxville, Tenn.

JEANETTE RASMUSSEN
John D. Pierce Junior High School
Redford, Mich.

SALLY RAYHILL
Harvest Park Middle School
Pleasanton, Calif.

JOANNE REHBERG
Northwood Junior High School
Spokane, Wash.

LYN REIMER
Traner Middle School
Reno, Nev.

KENNETH H. RINEAMAN
Matthew Henson Middle School
Indian Head, Md.

DIANNE RITCHEY
Parent Volunteer
Jonesboro, Ark.

STEWART D. ROBERSON
Walker-Grant Intermediate School
Fredericksburg, Va.

MARY ROBERTS
University of Tulsa
Tulsa, Okla.

DIANE A. ROCHESTER
University of N. Colorado
    Laboratory Middle School
Greeley, Colo.

SUSAN E. ROSENGRANT
Mahopac Junior High School
Mahopac, N.Y.

LOLYNN RYDZESKI
Louisville Middle School
Louisville, Colo.

SANDRA SCHURR
National Resource Center for
    Middle Grades Education
Tampa, Fla.

COLLEEN SETTJE
University of N. Colorado
    Laboratory Middle School
Greeley, Colo.

MARY SHEETZ
Cross Junior High School
Tucson, Ariz.

ARMENIA SMITH
Ysleta Independent School District
El Paso, Tex.

SHERRI SMITH
Roosevelt Junior High School
Newark, Ohio

GENE SODERQUIST
Alameda Junior High School
Pocatello, Idaho

SALLY J. SPORTSMAN
Raymore-Peculiar High School
Peculiar, Mo.

HAYWARD STEELE
DeRidder Junior High School
DeRidder, La.

DAVID R. STEPHENSON
Libby Junior High School
Libby, Mont.

TONY STRAKA
Keith Valley Middle School
Horsham, Penn.

JUDY SUTER
Alta Loma Elementary School
Alta Loma, Calif.

JUDY TASSIELLI
Omak Middle School
Omak, Wash.

BETTE TELLIER
Scott Carpenter Middle School
Denver, Colo.

JULIAN TORRES
Toppenish School District
Toppenish, Wash.

DOLORES C. URIAS
El Paso Independent
   School District
El Paso, Tex.

ALICE MCVETTY VARS
The School House
Kent, Ohio

CAROL WARREN
5 Oaks Intermediate School
Beaverton, Oreg.

AUDREY WERNER
Suzanne Middle School
Walnut, Calif.

JERRY J. WILCHER
Evans Middle School
Evans, Ga.

WILLIAM G. WISE
Benjamin Stoddert Middle School
Waldorf, Md.

PAT YOUNG
Woodmont Middle School
Piedmont, S.C.

CHERYL YOUNGER
Carroll County Middle School
Carrollton, Ky.

CLARE M. ZELENKA
John F. Kennedy Middle School
Redwood City, Calif.

Schools in Which Observations Took Place

ALCOA MIDDLE SCHOOL
Alcoa, Tenn.

ALEXANDER ELEMENTARY SCHOOL
Grand Rapids, Mich.

ALISAL ELEMENTARY SCHOOL
Pleasanton, Calif.

ALTA LOMA ELEMENTARY SCHOOL
Alta Loma, Calif.

ARNCO-SERGENT MIDDLE SCHOOL
Newnan, Ga.

ARROWHEAD ELEMENTARY SCHOOL
Aurora, Colo.

ARTHUR ELEMENTARY SCHOOL
Ceder Rapids, Iowa

BALDWIN INTERMEDIATE SCHOOL
Quincy, Ill.

BETHANY ELEMENTARY SCHOOL
Beaverton, Oreg.

BLAIR MIDDLE SCHOOL
Norfolk, Va.

HARVEY BOLICH MIDDLE SCHOOL
Cuyahoga Falls, Ohio

BOTHWELL MIDDLE SCHOOL
Marquette, Mich.

OMAR BRADLEY MIDDLE SCHOOL
San Antonio, Tex.

CALABASAS SCHOOL
Tumacacori, Ariz.

SCOTT CARPENTER MIDDLE SCHOOL
Denver, Colo.

CARROLL COUNTY MIDDLE SCHOOL
Carrollton, Ky.

CARVER ELEMENTARY SCHOOL
Milledgeville, Ga.

CARVER SIXTH GRADE SCHOOL
Waco, Tex.

CASHMERE MIDDLE SCHOOL
Cashmere, Wash.

CENTRAL SCHOOL
Glencoe, Ill.

131

CHATHAM MIDDLE SCHOOL
Chatham, N.J.

JOHNNY CLEM ELEMENTARY SCHOOL
Newark, Ohio

COLUMBIA MIDDLE SCHOOL
Champaign, Ill.

CORAL SPRINGS MIDDLE SCHOOL
Coral Springs, Fla.

CRESTWOOD MIDDLE SCHOOL
Mantua, Ohio

CUMBERLAND MIDDLE SCHOOL
Cumberland, R.I.

DEER CANYON ELEMENTARY SCHOOL
Alta Loma, Calif.

DEFOREST MIDDLE SCHOOL
DeForest, Ill.

DEL MAR MIDDLE SCHOOL
Santa Cruz, Calif.

DENALI ELEMENTARY SCHOOL
Fairbanks, Alaska

DERIDDER JUNIOR HIGH SCHOOL
DeRidder, La.

DOUGLAS ELEMENTARY SCHOOL
Garden City, Mich.

DOVER ELEMENTARY SCHOOL
Westlake, Ohio

GLENN DUNCAN ELEMENTARY
  SCHOOL
Reno, Nev.

EAGLEVIEW MIDDLE SCHOOL
Colorado Springs, Colo.

EASTWOOD HEIGHTS
El Paso, TX

EDGEMONT ELEMENTARY SCHOOL
Provo, Utah

EDISON MIDDLE SCHOOL
El Paso, Texas

EISENHOWER ELEMENTARY SCHOOL
Jacksonville, Ill.

EL DORADO MIDDLE SCHOOL
El Dorado, Kans.

FAIRVIEW ELEMENTARY SCHOOL
Carthage, Mo.

FALMOUTH MIDDLE SCHOOL
Falmouth, Maine

FISHER SCHOOL
Redford, Mich.

FORT LUPTON MIDDLE SCHOOL
Fort Lupton, Colo.

MILLS E. GODWIN MIDDLE SCHOOL
Woodbridge, Va.

GREENVILLE INTERMEDIATE SCHOOL
Greenville, Tex.

HAHIRA MIDDLE SCHOOL
Hahira, Ga.

HAVRE JUNIOR HIGH SCHOOL
Havre, Mont.

MATTHEW HENSON MIDDLE SCHOOL
Indian Head, Md.

HIGHLAND PARK ELEMENTARY
  SCHOOL
Oklahoma City, Okla.

HILLSDALE MIDDLE SCHOOL
Mobile, Ala.

HOOVER MIDDLE SCHOOL
Kenmore, N.Y.

HOWARD ELEMENTARY SCHOOL
Fremont, Nebr.

JENKS EAST MIDDLE SCHOOL
Jenks, Okla.

KEITH VALLEY MIDDLE SCHOOL
Horsham, Penn.

KENMORE MIDDLE SCHOOL
Kenmore, N.Y.

LADERA ELEMENTARY SCHOOL
Farmington, Maine

LAMAR MIDDLE SCHOOL
Lamar, Mo.

LEWIS & CLARK ELEMENTARY
SCHOOL
Pocatello, Idaho

LINCOLN ELEMENTARY SCHOOL
Jamestown, N. Dak.

LOMA TERRACE
El Paso, Tex.

LOS CERROS MIDDLE SCHOOL
Danville, Calif.

LOVELL MIDDLE SCHOOL
Lovell, Wyo.

MACARTHUR MIDDLE SCHOOL
El Paso, Tex.

MAHOPAC JUNIOR HIGH SCHOOL
Mahopac, N.Y.

MANASQUAN ELEMENTARY
SCHOOL
Manasquan, N.J.

MARTINEZ ELEMENTARY SCHOOL
Martinez, Ga.

MCKINLEY MIDDLE SCHOOL
Cedar Rapids, Iowa

MEADOWBROOK ELEMENTARY
SCHOOL
Waukesha, Wis.

MEMORIAL MIDDLE SCHOOL
Laconia, N.H.

MILLER ELEMENTARY SCHOOL
Newark, Ohio

MONTCLAIR ELEMENTARY
SCHOOL
Beaverton, Oreg.

MOORE MIDDLE SCHOOL
Tyler, Tex.

NEW CASTLE MIDDLE SCHOOL
New Castle, Del.

NORTH JUNIOR HIGH SCHOOL
Edinburg, Tex.

NORTH MIDDLE SCHOOL
Aurora, Colo.

UNIVERSITY OF N. COLORADO
LABORATORY MIDDLE SCHOOL
Greeley, Colo.

NORTHWEST MIDDLE SCHOOL
Knoxville, Tenn.

NOVAK ELEMENTARY SCHOOL
Marion, Iowa

NUUANU ELEMENTARY SCHOOL
Honolulu, Hawaii

J. W. O'BANION MIDDLE SCHOOL
Garland, Tex.

OMAK MIDDLE SCHOOL
Omak, Wash.

PATTONVILLE HEIGHTS MIDDLE
SCHOOL
Maryland Heights, Md.

PENNBROOK MIDDLE SCHOOL
North Wales, Penn.

PIERCE SCHOOL
Arlington, Mass.

POWELL MIDDLE SCHOOL
Powell, Tenn.

POWELL MIDDLE SCHOOL
Powell, Wyo.

PRAIRIE VIEW ELEMENTARY SCHOOL
Devils Lake, N. Dak.

RAYMORE-PECULIAR MIDDLE SCHOOL
Peculiar, Mo.

HENRY RUFF ELEMENTARY SCHOOL
Garden City, Mich.

GORDON RUSSELL MIDDLE SCHOOL
Gresham, Oreg.

S & S MIDDLE SCHOOL
Southmayd, Tex.

SARASOTA MIDDLE SCHOOL
Sarasota, Fla.

SAUK TRAIL
Middleton, Wis.

SAUNDERS MIDDLE SCHOOL
Woodbridge, Va.

SELBY LANE ELEMENTARY SCHOOL
Redwood City, Calif.

SHILOH ELEMENTARY SCHOOL
Spokane, Wash.

SINGER HIGH SCHOOL
Singer, La.

SOONER-ROSE ELEMENTARY SCHOOL
Midwest City, Okla.

SOUTH ELEMENTARY SCHOOL
Jonesboro, Ark.

SOUTHWEST SCHOOL
Waterford, Conn.

STEAD ELEMENTARY SCHOOL
Reno, Nev.

STERLING MIDDLE SCHOOL
Wenatchee, Wash.

BENJAMIN STODDERT MIDDLE
    SCHOOL
Waldorf, Md.

SUZANNE MIDDLE SCHOOL
Walnut, Calif.

THE SATZ SCHOOL
Holmdel, N.J.

TONALEA ELEMENTARY SCHOOL
Scottsdale, Ariz.

TOPPENISH MIDDLE SCHOOL
Toppenish, Wash.

TOWANDA ELEMENTARY SCHOOL
Towanda, Kans.

UNION PARK ELEMENTARY
    SCHOOL
Orlando, Fla.

UNIVERSITY PARK ELEMENTARY
    SCHOOL
Fairbanks, Alaska

WALKER GRANT INTERMEDIATE
    SCHOOL
Fredericksburg, Va.

WALNUT SPRINGS MIDDLE
    SCHOOL
Westerville, Ohio

WEST MIDDLETON ELEMENTARY
    SCHOOL
Verona, Wis.

WIDSTEN SCHOOL
Wayzata, Minn.

WINNISQUAM MIDDLE SCHOOL
Tilton, N.H.

ASA WOOD ELEMENTARY SCHOOL
Libby, Mont.

WOODBRIDGE MIDDLE SCHOOL
Woodbridge, Va.

WOODMONT MIDDLE SCHOOL
Piedmont, S.C.

WILBUR WRIGHT MIDDLE SCHOOL
Munster, Ind.

WYLIE MIDDLE SCHOOL
Wylie, Tex.

Analysts

Alfred A. Arth
University of Wyoming
Laramie, Wyo.

Edward Barnhart
Sterling Middle School
East Wenatchee, Wash.

Emma Lee Bass
Annie Camp Junior High School
Jonesboro, Ark.

Sherrel Bergmann
National College of Education
Evanston, Ill.

Joan Bloomer
Prince William County Public
Schools
Manassas, Va.

Terry Brooks
Jefferson County Public Schools
Louisville, Ky.

John Delaney
Parker Middle School
Reading, Mass.

Donald Eichhorn
Lewisburg Area School District
Lewisburg, Penn.

Thomas Erb
University of Kansas
Lawrence, Kans.

Carol Fillenberg
School District 50
Westminster, Colo.

Lucille Freeman
Kearney State College
Kearney, Maine

James Garvin
New England League of Middle
Schools
Rowley, Mass.

Joan Grady
Horizon Middle School
Aurora, Colo.

Larry Holt
University of Wisconsin
Platteville, Wis.

Linda Hopping
Holcomb Bridge Middle School
Alpharetta, Ga.

Laurel Kanthak
Suzanne Middle School
Walnut, Calif.

Edward Lawton
    College of Charleston
    Charleston, S.C.

Katie Sheppard
    Boddie Junior High School
    Milledgeville, Ga.

Lori Simmons
    Toppenish Middle School
    Toppenish, Wash.

David Strahan
    University of North Carolina
    Greensboro, N.C.

Conrad F. Toepfer, Jr.
    SUNY-Buffalo
    Amherst, N.Y.

John Van Hoose
    University of North Carolina
    Greensboro, N.C.

Ruth Walsh
    Washington Elementary School
    Laramie, Wyo.